C000214499

TERRY GAINER

When

TRAINS

RULED *the* KOOTENAYS

A Brief History of Railways

in Southeastern British Columbia

FOREWORD BY TOM LYMBERY

RMB

Copyright © 2022 by Terry Gainer
First Edition

For information on purchasing bulk quantities of this book, or to obtain media excerpts or invite the author to speak at an event, please visit rmbooks.com and select the "Contact" tab.

RMB | Rocky Mountain Books Ltd.
rmbooks.com
@rmbooks
facebook.com/rmbooks

Cataloguing data available from Library and Archives Canada
ISBN 9781771604017 (paperback)
ISBN 9781771604024 (electronic)

Printed and bound in Canada by Friesens

We would like to also take this opportunity to acknowledge the traditional territories upon which we live and work. In Calgary, Alberta, we acknowledge the Niitsítapi (Blackfoot) and the people of the Treaty 7 region in Southern Alberta, which includes the Siksika, the Piikuni, the Kainai, the Tsuut'ina, and the Stoney Nakoda First Nations, including Chiniki, Bearpaw, and Wesley First Nations. The City of Calgary is also home to Métis Nation of Alberta, Region III. In Victoria, British Columbia, we acknowledge the traditional territories of the Lkwungen (Esquimalt and Songhees), Malahat, Pacheedaht, Scia'new, T'Sou-ke, and W̱SÁNEĆ (Pauquachin, Tsartlip, Tsawout, Tseycum) peoples.

All rights reserved. No part of this publication may be reproduced, stored in a retrieval system, or transmitted in any form or by any means – electronic, mechanical, audio recording, or otherwise – without the written permission of the publisher or a photocopying licence from Access Copyright. Permissions and licensing contribute to a secure and vibrant book industry by helping to support writers and publishers through the purchase of authorized editions and excerpts. To obtain an official licence, please visit accesscopyright.ca or call 1-800-893-5777.

We acknowledge the financial support of the Government of Canada through the Canada Book Fund and the Canada Council for the Arts, and of the province of British Columbia through the British Columbia Arts Council and the Book Publishing Tax Credit.

I am proud to dedicate this book to my grandson Bjorn, the most recent addition to the Gainer clan. Bjorn, when my loving daughter Chantal brought you into this world, you gave my life a whole new dimension. Now I have another reason to live and love.

Nothing is too small to know,
and nothing is too big to attempt.

—*William Cornelius Van Horne, president and chairman,*
board of directors, Canadian Pacific Railway

Most men who have really lived have had, in some share,
their great adventure. This railway is mine.

—*James J. Hill, founder and president,*
Great Northern Railway

TABLE OF CONTENTS

FOREWORD

BY TOM LYMBERY

Terry Gainer grew up watching passenger trains bring crowds of people to Banff. The Gainer family lived above the Canadian Pacific Railway (CPR) station, as Terry's father was the station agent. As a child, Terry's ambition was to be a redcap, a job he secured as soon as he turned 16. Terry worked at the Banff station for the next six summers, providing the background for his first book, *When Trains Ruled the Rockies*.

Terry's fascination with the railways of the Kootenays began in the mid '90s when he arrived in Trail as managing partner of Dewdney Coach Lines. He positioned Dewdney as a successful charter operation that served the Kootenays from Fernie to Grand Forks, Golden to Cranbrook and Trail to Nelson to Nakusp. He travelled extensively throughout the region. "Everywhere you go, you'd see the remains of the railway infrastructure, and as a train lover, it tweaked my imagination." I'm sure his travels planted the seed for this book.

Rail books are popular, but nearly all are about rail operation and construction, with little information about passengers and schedules. Terry's books fill a most necessary need as all travellers have stories to tell–about the people they met and the scenery they enjoyed.

Because of the long lakes to be crossed to travel the Kootenays, the connections necessarily included barges, tugs and sternwheelers for passengers–even rail lines whose only link to other rails was by water. The longest-lasting operation of train and barge was the Slocan City to Rosebery route. The entire train would be loaded onto a barge, sail the length of Slocan Lake then unload back onto the rails to Nakusp. That attracted rail buffs and photographers for years.

Moving to Canada from England, my parents spent days travelling across Canada from Halifax, passing through the Rockies over the Crowsnest Pass, arriving at Kootenay Landing. Then they boarded a comfortable sternwheeler, a five-hour trip to Nelson, BC. The next day they would finally travel to Gray Creek on the SS *Moyie*. The entire journey, booked and paid for before leaving England, was possible because "The CPR spanned the world back in the day." Even at the CPR ticket office on Baker Street in Nelson, you could book anywhere in the world by CP rail, steamship and hotel.

But Terry's book expands on the intense competition from the US—the Great Northern, whose rails came north of the border to tap into the rich mines in Rossland, Slocan and Boundary. US rail baron and magnate James J. Hill financed the narrow-gauge line from Kaslo to Sandon and operated a fleet of sternwheelers on Kootenay Lake. Battles between rail workers broke out at various construction sites, including Sandon.

The Great Northern brought its rails across the border through Creston to a landing at Kuskanook, meeting the CPR heading for Kootenay Landing in 1898. Limited right-of-way along the lake's east shore required that they share trackage for an eight-mile stretch. It was one of the few instances of cooperation during that era. In a few short years, the town of Kuskanook went from boom to bust.

Before the advent of paved roads in the 1950s, travelling on polished steel rails with connections to the sternwheeler fleets was much more comfortable than the gravel highways that produced the constant washboard effect. Passenger trains ruled, and Terry covers this ground well.

Terry found researching the Kootenays captivating and located many previously unpublished photographs that will appear in the book. This title will appeal to more readers than just dedicated rail buffs. I expect this publication will receive even more awards than his previous work.

PREFACE

In the 1890s, the transcontinental railways of North America were racing across the country, feverishly building new lines to access the vast mineral and timber resources in western Canada and the Pacific Northwest. Often two or more railways were locked in fierce competition to exploit the same regions. Confrontations were the order of the day, as control of territory could lead to vastly increased revenues.

The strategies and tactics were numerous, often less than honourable, as the competitors fought to win right-of-way monopolies, thereby controlling resource development. With competitors out of the way, the company could impose iron-clad contracts on new developing industries. When political favours and influence faltered, the option was to control the transportation landscape by ownership of everything in the supply chain; from purchasing connecting steamboat services on inland waterways, buying up the smelters, coal mines and mining leases, or, as a last resort, using violence.

The competition for dominance in southeastern British Columbia was no exception. In the 1880s, rich coal deposits had been discovered in the Crowsnest Pass, extending from Frank and Blairmore in Alberta to Fernie in British Columbia's East Kootenay. In the West Kootenay, the game changer occurred in 1887, when two brothers, Osner and Winslow Hall, discovered a silver deposit at their Silver King claim near Nelson that was so rich the continent erupted in a frenzy, and the rush was on. The hysteria continued through the 1890s, when prospectors struck copper ore in Boundary County, adjoining the West Kootenay. Barrie Sanford, author of the railway masterpiece *McCulloch's Wonder: The Story of the Kettle Valley Railway*, sums it up best. "The location was all that was needed to be known. Within hours, the first American had crossed the boundary into Canada, staking his claim in the Kootenays, and thousands more were on his heels."[1] A titanic struggle for control of the Kootenays was about to begin!

1   Barrie Sanford, *McCulloch's Wonder: The Story of the Kettle Valley Railway* (Vancouver: Whitecap Books, 1988), 15.

ACKNOWLEDGEMENTS

I think it would be impossible to write a book on your own. I have so many people to thank for their assistance, and I don't know what I would have done without them. I left writing the acknowledgements to the end of the project, terrified I'd forget to mention someone. This book covers a lot of ground, and so did I during the researching process. At every stop along the way, I encountered unstinting assistance and genuine hospitality.

My thanks begin with Tom Lymbery, the eminent Kootenay entrepreneur, historian and author. Tom, born in 1928, was raised and still lives at Gray Creek on the east shore of Kootenay Lake. Arthur Lymbery, Tom's father, was a true Kootenay pioneer and established the iconic Gray Creek Store, carried on by Tom until 2011. Now his son David, the third generation Lymbery, has succeeded him, operating the store. From the beginning, Tom understood where I wanted to go with this book. He provided sound advice and pointed the way when at one point I felt myself floundering. His anecdotes and experiences allowed me to add a human touch and depth to the manuscript that I could not duplicate. When Tom offered to write the foreword, I was deeply honoured. Tom, I cannot thank you enough.

As with my first book, the support I've received from my daughter is paramount. Chantal, you are my best cheerleader and always there for me. The encouragement I receive from my sisters, Sylvia and Frances, brother, Fred, and wife, Connie, fuel the fire.

I spent hours in archives around the Kootenays, researching books and newspaper articles, searching for photographs and other historical documents to maintain historical accuracy and integrity. The assistance I received from staff and volunteers at all the archives visited astounds me. There is something about folks who dedicate their time to preserving history. I encountered sincere interest and cooperation everywhere I called. In particular, I want to thank the following individuals:

In Nelson, J.P. Stienne, curator of Touchstones Museum of Art and History, his staff and volunteers must have thought I intended to move in! For over a year, I visited the archives almost daily. There are no words to thank you for your patience and assistance during my searches, especially for historical images.

Elizabeth Scarlett, archivist at the Kootenay Lake Historical Society, and her able assistant, Florence Woods, definitely went the extra mile for me in my quest for images of early Kaslo trains, stations and sternwheelers. The pictures you found for me make my book come to life.

Kyle Kusch, archivist at the Arrow Lakes Historical Society, is no stranger to the publishing world, having published the award-winning book *Our Coloured Past: The Arrow Lakes in the Age of Colour Photography*. Kyle, I cannot thank you enough for helping me choose the best images in your collection for my book.

I met Jesslyn Jarvis, collections coordinator, at the Trail Museum in the summer of 2020. Jesslyn introduced me to the *Trail Creek Times* and the early history of Trail's railways and smelter, plus sourcing some incredible photos. My sincere thanks for your help. Jesslyn has since moved on, and I wish her all the best in her future endeavours.

Addison Oberg became my other guiding light in Trail, succeeding Jesslyn as collections coordinator. My photo selection was incomplete, and Addison dug out rare photos of the Cominco Annual Picnic I had given up on locating. Thank you, Addison.

Sarah Taekema is research manager, and Sara Wright is collections manager at the Rossland Museum & Discovery Centre, custodians of the *Rossland Miner* newspaper back into the early 1890s that documents the birth of Rossland. The *Miner* became my best source for the history of the 1890s era. I am deeply indebted to Sarah and Sara for accommodating me, often on short notice, and assisting me in prowling through the files.

Mel Billings of Nakusp introduced me to the Nakusp Rail Society, which brought to light information I could never have sourced on my own. Mel, an associate from the 1980s in the Canadian Rockies, introduced me to Kyle Kusch and the Arrow Lakes Historical Society. Many, many thanks, Mel.

The "crack" passenger train in North America in the early 1900s was the Soo-Spokane Train Deluxe, from Saint Paul and Minneapolis to Spokane through the Crowsnest Pass route. I was fortunate to contact Emory Luebke at the Soo Line Historical and Technical Society. While I had some basic information about the train, Emory provided a gold mine of crucial details, including the original 1907 schedule and photographs of the train passing through North Dakota to Moose Jaw, Saskatchewan, the CPR main line. Emory, I'm deeply indebted.

David Humphrey is a volunteer at the Cranbrook History Centre, home to the Soo-Spokane Train Deluxe and the Trans-Canada Limited. David went beyond the call of duty, sourcing information on the first Soo-Spokane arrival in Cranbrook and an outstanding photograph of the train at the Cranbrook station. Thanks again, David.

When I decided to add the section on the trains of the Kootenays, I picked the bellwether year of 1906 to describe the train and sternwheeler transportation network. And hit a wall. I found schedules from newspapers and journals, but none of them were of any particular year, let alone 1906. Hoping my rail buff pal, Steve Boyko, might be able to help, I sent a desperate email. Steve replied, "No problem, Terry," directing me to his website, www.traingeek.ca. There it was, a schedule from 1906. Steve, you've done it again!

Chantal Guérin is an archival technician at Exporail, the Canadian Railway Museum in Montreal. Chantal was able to source from the CPR archives copies of the 1916, 1930 and 1931 timetables for the Crowsnest and Kootenay lines, including the "Crow Boats." As well, she located quality photos of the Kootenay Express and the Crowsnest station. Thank you for the great finds, Chantal. The information was essential for a couple of chapters.

I've never had the pleasure of meeting Barrie Sanford, author of *McCulloch's Wonder: The Story of the Kettle Valley Railway*. Without a doubt, it is the best railway history I've ever read– my "go-to" reference. Thanks, Barrie, and belated congratulations. I'm hopeful our paths will cross one day.

David Love, president of the Canadian Pacific Historical Association, introduced me to Stephen Sadis, president of Great Northern Filmworks, and producer and director of the documentary *The Empire Builder: The Story of James J. Hill & the Great Northern Railway*. Stephen approached me to interview for his documentary on David's recommendation, as I had some historical knowledge of the CPR and the Great Northern conflict in Canada. In preparation for the interview, Stephen provided me with volumes of information about Great Northern and James J. Hill, his early years and his relationship with the CPR. Stephen and his film crew interviewed me in

Spokane in 2019. That was the genesis of *When Trains Ruled the Kootenays*. Stephen, you were an inspiration, and I left that interview with a seed germinating in my mind. David, many thanks for bringing us together. Had I not met Stephen, this book wouldn't exist.

I first visited the Japanese Canadian internment camp in New Denver back in the 1990s. I was astounded at this piece of Canadian history. It was not a part of any history class during my school years. But until I connected with Kaien and Henry Shimizu, internees at the camp from 1942 to 1946, I had no idea of the depth of racism and hypocrisy of the BC and federal governments of the day. I am indebted to Kaien and Henry for sharing their emotional experiences of an unpleasant part of their past. Thank you for your recollections and your candid comments in the course of our discussions.

Don Gorman is the publisher at Rocky Mountain Books, without whom I'd be unpublished (and probably unpublishable). He's also a pretty awesome guy. Don, you've guided me through the minefields of the book world, and I'm still shaking my head, two books later, that this all happened for me. You are the reason, and I'll owe you forever! Thank you a thousand times.

INTRODUCTION

When Trains Ruled the Kootenays is a story of the railways that conquered the rugged landscapes of the Kootenays, spearheading the settlement and development of southeastern British Columbia. For the successful entrepreneurs, the stakes were high, and the major railways in the West were on the move to exploit the riches of the new "Eldorado." The Kootenays exploded in a battle for dominance.

Part 1 details the colourful and tumultuous history of the railway incursions into southeastern British Columbia, introducing the main antagonists in the "Battle for the Kootenays." Railway legend William Cornelius Van Horne led the Canadian Pacific (CP), the Great Northern (GN) was led by founder and president, James J. Hill, and the Spokane Falls & Northern Railway by Daniel Corbin, Spokane's famous railway baron, builder of the first railway into the Kootenays from the United States. None of these men were short on ambition, talent or ego; for over 20 years, they repeatedly clashed while simultaneously taming the rugged landscape and building fleets of sternwheelers to harness the inland waterways. But this is not another book detailing railway construction and maintenance in British Columbia. Excellent books are available on that subject, and I refer to them often.

Part 2 focuses on the unique marriage of rail and water transportation that connected the Kootenay communities. In conversation with eminent Kootenay historian and author Tom Lymbery, he noted, "Many books are available about the construction and operating problems of the Kootenay railways, but it is rare to find anything about passenger travel on these routes." Passenger trains and passenger travel are the focus of Part 2.

The railway builders of the Kootenays were unique; they understood that vertical integration of their companies was the key to success, if not outright monopoly. Aside from being railways, both the Canadian Pacific and the Great Northern owned smelters and mines in the supply chain. Both operated a sternwheeler fleet, and Daniel Corbin built a company town in the Crowsnest Pass for his coal mine and miners. "Intermodal" train and steamboat connections began to change the north–south flow of river transportation from Canada to the USA to an east–west traffic flow, allowing Canadians and new immigrants easy access to settlements and opportunities in British Columbia's southern interior.

To maintain historical accuracy, I have drawn on archival information from the Cranbrook, Nelson, Arrow Lakes, Kootenay Lake, Rossland and Trail museums and archives. Much of the human history comes from newspaper files dating back to the 1890s, interviews with long-time residents and facts, scraps and anecdotes from locals, who, along with their parents, actually lived and experienced life during this formative and colourful era.

On a personal note, my passion for passenger rail began at an early age, when our family moved to Banff, Alberta, in 1948. The CPR had appointed my dad, F.L. (Frank) Gainer, station agent, and the position included a two-bedroom residence on top of the train station. I could almost reach out and touch the arriving and departing passengers, only feet below on the platform. Thus began my lifelong love affair with trains, which eventually led me to write my first book, *When Trains Ruled the Rockies*, published in 2019. Hopefully, this publication opens the door to understanding the importance of the Kootenay region to British Columbia and Canada as it burst upon the world stage.

PART I
Rails to the Kootenays

THE KOOTENAYS

The Kootenays cover approximately nine million hectares (35,000 square miles) in the southeastern corner of British Columbia. The Arrow Lakes to the west, the top of the Columbia Basin north of Revelstoke, and the Rocky Mountains to the east and south to the US border frame the region. Further subdivided, the East Kootenay extends from the Alberta border to the west slope of the Purcell Mountains. The West Kootenay extends from the Selkirk Mountains bordering on Kootenay Lake to Arrow Lakes. Historically, the Crowsnest Pass through the Rockies to Fernie provided the best access to enter the East Kootenay region from the Canadian prairies.

But the mountain ranges of western Canada and the USA run north to south, defying the east–west international boundary. The rivers through the mountain ranges were the Kootenay region's logical transportation routes. The Kootenay River flows from the west slopes of the Canadian Rockies, then dips down into the USA, before turning north at Bonners Ferry, Idaho, back into Canada and forming Kootenay Lake, a massive freshwater sea. Over 100 km long, Kootenay Lake is located in the valley between the Purcell and the Selkirk mountain ranges and had served as a water highway for Indigenous Peoples for hundreds of years before the arrival of European explorers and fur traders.

The outlet flow from the lake meets the Columbia River west of Nelson at what is now Castlegar, BC. The Columbia, also rising on the west slopes of the Rockies, flows from Columbia Lake near Fairmont Hot Springs north past Golden, BC, and then swings south to Revelstoke, through eastern Washington and Oregon, emptying into the Pacific Ocean at Astoria, OR. Before the 1880s, the Kootenays was the domain of Indigenous Peoples and American traders and prospectors, who roamed freely across the border. But the reported discovery of vast silver and copper deposits by Oscar and Winslow Hall on Toad Mountain changed the landscape.

In 1887 the Americans poured into the Kootenays. The proximity of the Northern Pacific Railroad, completed in 1883, brought prospectors and opportunists by the thousands, who then took riverboats or rafts and canoes on the Columbia and Kootenay rivers to Canada. Nelson, a new settlement, was overflowing. Prospectors from all walks of life established mining camps on the shores of Kootenay Lake.

Then, in 1890, two prospectors from Dewdney Trail discovered gold, and the Le Roi mine was born. A man named Major Topping purchased the claim for the filing fee of $12.50 and then flipped it for $30,000 to a Spokane, Washington, mining consortium. It became Rossland's largest producer. A gold rush was on, and Rossland exploded. By 1897 the population had reached 7,000 residents, with more on the way. But little of the mined ore stayed in Canada as Kootenay riches flowed south to established smelters in Coeur d'Alene and Spokane. Politicians from Victoria to Ottawa took up the cry for a railway across southern BC.

The main line of the CPR, completed in 1885, touched on the top end of the Kootenays at Revelstoke, but there was no "southern" access. However, the discovery of gold and silver soon spurred the railways into action. The federal and BC governments granted multiple charters; some built, but many never left the planning stage. By 1900 the major players had established competing railways and steamboat services that criss-crossed the Kootenays, leading to intense competition and often open conflict. Southern British Columbia became a railway battleground, and the Kootenays were on the front line.

THE ANTAGONISTS

I have driven thousands of kilometres criss-crossing the Kootenays, tracing and following the rail lines that once blanketed the landscape and discovering pilings and decaying structures of the landings and docks that were once home to the tugs and the majestic lake sternwheelers. I still have difficulty grappling with the incredible feats of construction that happened over 100 years ago without the aid of today's earthmovers, sophisticated drilling machinery and modern explosives. Picks, shovels, men and dynamite, aided by horse-drawn wagons, always seemed to me as a pittance in the arsenal you'd require when setting out to conquer the rugged mountain terrain in British Columbia. But even more remarkable were the men who led the charge across the continent to conquer the Kootenays. Were they Supermen? None had college educations, yet they were the foremost builders in our nation's history. All of their training and education seems to have happened on the job. There is no doubt they were born leaders.

The *Dictionary of Canadian Biography* introduces three antagonists in the "Battle for the Kootenays."[2] They were all

2   The three being William Cornelius Van Horne, James Jerome Hill and Daniel Corbin. See Theodore D. Regehr, "VAN HORNE, Sir WILLIAM CORNELIUS," in Dictionary of Canadian Biography, vol. 14, University of Toronto/Université Laval, 2003–, http://www.biographi. ca/en/bio/van_horne_william_cornelius_14E.html; David G. Burley, "HILL, JAMES JEROME," in Dictionary of Canadian Biography, vol. 14, University of Toronto/Université Laval, 2003–, http://www.biographi.

driven to succeed, and their intense competition led to frequent clashes and ill feelings. Often their dogged determination and unwillingness to compromise led to a duplication of services. As a result, the province of British Columbia was often the beneficiary, resulting in accelerated development and settlement in the province's interior.

William Cornelius Van Horne rose from general manager to president and eventually chairman of the board for the Canadian Pacific Railway. On February 3, 1843, Van Horne was born near Chelsea, Illinois. At the age of 11, his father died, forcing him to help support the family. His formal schooling ended at age 14, when he was punished for drawing and circulating dubious caricatures of his principal. He never went back.

He began his railway career as a telegrapher with the Illinois Central Railroad, first becoming a ticket agent before eventually rising to divisional superintendent in 1862 with the Chicago and Alton Railroad. After overseeing the acquisitions of two other railroads, he became general manager. In 1879 Van Horne became general superintendent of the Chicago, Milwaukee, St. Paul & Pacific Railroad, later known as the "Milwaukee Road."

At this point, Van Horne's career brought him into contact with James Jerome Hill, Minnesota's most aggressive and successful railroader. In 1880 George Stephen, president of the Bank of Montreal, and his cousin, Donald Smith, convinced Hill to join the Canadian Pacific Syndicate. The syndicate then signed a massive contract with the Canadian government to

ca/en/bio/hill_james_jerome_14E.html; and Jeremy Mouat, "CORBIN, DANIEL CHASE," in Dictionary of Canadian Biography, vol. 14, University of Toronto/Université Laval, 2003–, http://www.biographi.ca/en/bio/corbin_daniel_chase_14E.html.

build the Pacific Railway. Hill engaged two experienced builders, Alpheus Stickney as general superintendent of western construction and Thomas Rosser as chief engineer. However, their
results were disappointing. Under pressure from Hill, Stickney
and Rosser resigned, and Hill recommended Van Horne to
manage the construction of the Canadian Pacific Railway. Hill
had written Stephen, the chairman, "I have never met anyone
who is better informed in various departments." Hill had lured
Van Horne to the CPR by offering one of the highest railway
salaries paid at the time, and Van Horne accepted.

As general manager, Van Horne was the engine that drove the
CPR to its completion with the "Last Spike" at Craigellachie,
BC, in 1885. In 1886 he was elected to the board of directors and
named vice-president. In 1888, when George Stephen resigned,
Van Horne became president. Leading the railway into a period
of expansion and through the chaos of the 1893 depression, Van
Horne established CP Hotels, a chain of luxury hotels across
Canada, and Canadian Pacific Steamships. Canadian Pacific
truly "spanned the world."

James Jerome Hill was the founder and president of the
Great Northern Railway. Hill was born on September 16, 1838,
in Eramosa Township, near Guelph, a farming community in
Upper Canada, now Ontario. Like Van Horne, Hill had a trou-
bling start in life. An accident blinded him in one eye at age 9,
and his education was cut short at age 14 by his father's death.
Hill, like Van Horne, left school to find work with his family
pressed for money. Eventually, Hill found better employment
opportunities in the United States, accepting a clerkship with
a shipping firm in Saint Paul, Minnesota, on the Mississippi
River. Hill was a quick study, and in 1865 established a freight
and forwarding business and built a warehouse on the St. Paul

and Pacific Railroad line. An agreement in 1867 gave him control of the line's riverside facilities, where he developed a coal trading company, negotiating purchases and freight charges to achieve greater profits, and dominated the market.

Hill foresaw that the settlement of the Canadian west would increase commerce through Saint Paul, the key trade centre en route to the Red River Colony in Manitoba. In 1872 Hill and Norman Kittson formed the Red River Transportation Company, and by 1877 the company was operating seven steamboats on the Red and Assiniboine rivers. But Hill had already decided that railways were the future: "In 1869, Hill had met Hudson's Bay Company officer Donald Smith in St. Paul. They met again in a makeshift winter camp the following year while en route to Fort Garry in the Red River Colony. These meetings were the genesis of Hill's involvement with Smith, George Stephen and the CPR Syndicate."[3]

When Smith visited in 1873–74, he proposed to Hill and Kittson to acquire St. Paul and Pacific Railroad, then in receivership, with an incomplete line to Manitoba. Without sufficient funds, Hill and Kittson assigned their holdings in Red River Transportation to Smith and his cousin George Stephen, a founder and president of the Bank of Montreal. In 1878 the associates had finished the line to the border. On May 23, a new entity, the St. Paul, Minneapolis and Manitoba Railway Company, began operation, with George Stephen as president, Kittson as vice-president and Hill as general manager. Hill would become president in 1883.

3   Stephen Sadis Research Information, Great Northern Filmworks, Seattle, WA, research files from The Empire Builder: The Story of James J. Hill & the Great Northern Railway. Courtesy Stephen Sadis, producer.

In 1880, after repeated overtures from Smith and Stephen, Hill agreed to join the CPR syndicate. Because Hill was too busy to supervise the westward construction, he recruited highly respected William Cornelius Van Horne of the Chicago, Milwaukee and St. Paul Railroad. Nothing, however, reduced his apprehensions about the CPR.

As the CPR built west, Hill complained about how construction materials tied up his rolling stock. In 1882 he objected when the Manitoba Line, contrary to its charter but on President George Stephen's instruction, purchased the Manitoba South-Western Colonization Railway to protect the CPR monopoly. In addition, he resented the fact that not only had Smith and Stephen reduced their Manitoba Line stock, but he found he had to pledge his shares to secure loans for the CPR. But the final straw for Hill was the decision by the CPR to build an all-Canadian route across the top of Lake Superior instead of a dip into the US at Duluth, Minnesota, connecting to existing trackage he owned, to Saint Paul and Winnipeg. "This decision resulted in a collision with Van Horne, who backed the all-Canadian route to Hill's surprise. Hill was enraged that his hand-picked lieutenant would oppose him, thus planting the seeds of the feud that would engulf both men for the next 30 years."[4] By 1883 Hill had had enough, resigning from the board and severing his ties with the Canadian Pacific Syndicate.

Hill then plunged ahead with his transcontinental vision. In 1885–86, he allied with the Chicago, Burlington and Quincy Railroad, revoking an agreement not to invade the territory of the Northern Pacific Railroad. By 1888 Hill had pushed a line into Montana, and, in 1889, boldly decided to carry on to the

4   Sadis, *The Empire Builder.*

Pacific. On January 6, 1893, Hill's "Last Spike" was driven, connecting Puget Sound with Saint Paul and Duluth, Minnesota.

Hill's main line through northern Montana, Idaho and Washington ran close to the Canadian border. With the significant mineral discoveries in the Kootenays, Hill saw an ideal opportunity to challenge his former company (and now nemesis) for dominance in the mining boom of British Columbia. Thus began one of the most riveting confrontations in railroading history. When they first met, Hill and Van Horne were close business associates, considered friends and allies. But over time they repeatedly clashed as they led their respective companies into the 20th century. Mutually respected business partners became bitter enemies as they fought head to head to control the Kootenays.

Daniel Corbin was the founder and president of Spokane Falls & Northern Railway, the Nelson & Fort Sheppard Railway and the Spokane International Railway. Born on October 1, 1832, in Newport, New Hampshire, in 1852 he joined the flood of Americans to the "Wild West" and found a position as a surveyor in the Iowa and Nebraska territories. But the beginning of his railway career took him back east to New York, working with his brother Austin, who owned the New York and Manhattan Railway, establishing Coney Island as a resort. In the 1880s, Corbin again headed west, following the construction of the Northern Pacific Railway in 1883. With the discovery of silver near Coeur d'Alene, Idaho, he constructed his first railway, the Coeur d'Alene Railway & Navigation Company, in 1886, then sold to the Northern Pacific for a hefty profit.

Attracted by the discovery of rich gold, silver and galena deposits in the Kootenays, Corbin shifted his focus to Canada. From his experience with the Coeur d'Alene railway, he understood the profitability of constructing feeder lines from the mines to the expanding transcontinental rail networks. The Canadian government initially rebuffed Corbin's application (with substantial pressure from the CPR) to build a rail line from Spokane to the Kootenays. BC entrepreneurs who stood to benefit successfully presented his second application. In December of 1893, the Nelson & Fort Sheppard Railway was completed from the border to Nelson and Kootenay Lake, connecting to the Spokane Falls & Northern Railway to Spokane. Over the next decade, Corbin built two more branch lines connecting southeastern British Columbia with Spokane Falls (Spokane), including the 17-mile branch line from Northport, Washington, to Rossland, BC.

Barrie Sanford writes that, by early 1897,

> Corbin noted unusual activity in the purchase of shares in his railroads. Initially, he suspected this might be the CPR attempting to control his railways. He inquired of J.P. Morgan, the famous US Banker and Financier, to identify the source of the stock purchases and start repurchasing shares on his behalf to protect the company. But unknown to Corbin, Morgan informed the mystery buyer, none other than James J. Hill of the Great Northern, that Corbin was preparing to buy large blocks of shares to retain control of his companies. Through Morgan, Hill quickly purchased the controlling interest. Within a year, Corbin was gone. He was infuriated but powerless to retaliate.[5]

As Jeremy Mouat writes in the *Dictionary of Canadian Biography*, "Corbin's railways had shaped the early development

5   Sanford, *McCulloch's Wonder*, 38.

of the Kootenays, establishing Spokane as the commercial centre of Washington, Idaho, and southeastern British Columbia. His career is illustrative of the American competition that forced the CPR to defend its interests in Western Canada, leading to the construction of the Crowsnest Pass line."[6]

Corbin faded away but did not disappear, reappearing with a vengeance in 1906 to build the Spokane International Railway. The Corbin–CPR alliance broke Hill's monopoly into Spokane and the Inland Empire markets of Washington state, eking out a measure of revenge against Hill, his long-time nemesis.

The famous proverb "The enemy of my enemy is my friend" was penned as far back as 400 BC. But it proved dead on during the "Battle of the Titans" that played out in the Kootenays between Van Horne, Hill and Corbin. Their intertwining histories and the skullduggery are legendary. Let the battle begin!

6 Mouat, "CORBIN, DANIEL CHASE."

THE BATTLE BEGINS: RAILS TO THE WEST KOOTENAYS

Daniel Chase Corbin built the first American railway into the Kootenays. Fully cognizant of the rich silver strikes and coal deposits in the Kootenays, he knew profits were there for the taking if he could connect a feeder line to the Northern Pacific in Spokane from the new mining discoveries in the Kootenays. In 1889 Corbin chartered the Spokane Falls & Northern Railway, and by 1890 the line was complete from Spokane to Little Dalles, just south of the Canadian border on the Columbia River. Barges delivered the ore from the Canadian mines to the railhead for shipment to Spokane area smelters.

Corbin then applied to the Canadian government to extend his rail line to Nelson and Kootenay Lake. At this point, Corbin's twisted web began to weave. The British Columbia government was concerned his request only served American interests in Spokane. Federally, British Columbia Member of Parliament John Mara vociferously opposed Corbin's request. Ottawa denied the charter. (A couple of years later, Mara would to do an about-turn.) Additionally, William Cornelius Van Horne, president of the CPR, informed the prime minister that his company opposed Corbin's application, stating the CPR would construct a rail line into the Kootenays if refused. It appeared that the CPR had finally stepped up to bat at the "Kootenay" plate.

Completing the Spokane Falls & Northern Railway to Little Dalles spurred the CPR. Sensing a deteriorating position for its plan to dominate transportation in the Kootenays, Canadian

Pacific finally commenced construction on its rail line. In 1890 executive Harry Abbott successfully applied to the BC government for his Columbia & Kootenay Railway charter. Abbott then leased it to the CPR for 999 years. In the spring of 1891, CPR's first train rolled into Nelson.

The CPR strategy was to build the rail line from Nelson to Robson, bypassing the unnavigable waters of the Kootenay River, hauling Nelson's ore and passengers to the CP wharf at Sproat's Landing (Robson) on the Columbia River. From that point, CPR steamboats and barges navigated north via Arrow Lakes and the Columbia River to the main line at Revelstoke, with connections to Vancouver and eastern Canada. A new smelter was built in Revelstoke, attempting to divert the flow of ore away from Spokane. On paper it sounded feasible, but Mother Nature was not always a willing partner. Frequently in winter, parts of Arrow Lakes became icebound, and in summer it was an expensive upstream battle for the steamboats. While the passenger service prospered, the smelter failed. Canadian Pacific could lay claim to the first railway in the Kootenays, but as Van Horne eventually conceded, the Columbia and Kootenay did little to advance CP's position. It was a stopgap solution to show the flag, avoid a significant cash outlay and buy some time.

It was back to the drawing board for the CPR, because Daniel Corbin was on the move.

Corbin had learned a valuable lesson in his first approach to the Canadian and BC governments; in the future, he would include Canadian executives to front his application to allay fears that the railroad would only be a feed to Spokane. Under his name, he then submitted an additional application in 1892, promising to build a second rail line through southern

BC along the Kettle River to Vancouver. The BC government roundly refused this application. It had caused such a stir in the local political scene that the Nelson & Fort Sheppard line application, fronted by BC executives, slipped through with little notice and received approval. In a startling turnaround, Corbin's most vocal supporter for the Kootenay line was the same federal MP, John Mara, who had so vociferously opposed his first application in 1890. Coincidentally (of course), and shortly after Corbin's first application for a rail charter, Mara became a financial partner in the Columbia and Kootenay Steam Navigation Company (CKSN), making a small fortune hauling ore to Corbin's railhead on the Columbia River. Mara now deemed Corbin's application to extend his rail line to Nelson "good for British Columbia." In December 1893, the Nelson & Fort Sheppard Railway commenced operations, complete to Five Mile Point, where Corbin built a railway terminal and wharf for easy connections with the Kootenay Lake steamboats. Probably not by coincidence, the newly expanded fleet of steamboats and barges of John Mara's Columbia and Kootenay Steam Navigation Company were on hand to meet the Nelson & Fort Sheppard at Five Mile Point, ready to haul ore from the Kootenay Lake mines in even greater volumes. Corbin's railways had proven to be a genuine threat. But the CPR was about to rejoin the fray, playing hardball by calling in political favours and then finally commencing construction of competing rail lines in the Kootenays.

When Corbin's Nelson & Fort Sheppard line approached the overlook above Nelson, Canadian Pacific fired its second shot with a political "waterfront ploy" designed to keep Corbin's railway out of the Nelson townsite. A CPR land agent presented Corbin's foreman with an official document issued by

British Columbia Premier John Robson. The certificate granted the CPR exclusive access to all Kootenay Lake foreshore land within the Nelson city limits. That effectively killed Corbin's plans for a Nelson terminus and easy access to the Silver King mine. CP had hoped this action would stop construction, forcing Corbin into negotiations. But to no avail. Without hesitation, Corbin made a snap decision, electing to bypass the CPR lakefront reserve, establishing the Mountain Station above the townsite, and then drove the rail line north to Five Mile Point on the west arm of Kootenay Lake. The terminal and boat landing at Five Mile became a permanent fixture, providing a seamless link to Spokane and the US smelters for the high-grade minerals of the Kootenays.

The CPR's blockade did not thwart Corbin by keeping his railway out of Nelson. By the end of 1894, he had laid track along the lake back towards town. Unable to enter the city centre, he built his so-called Nelson station on the edge of the CPR waterfront tract, about a mile north of downtown. "It didn't take long for the local press, often an ally of the CPR, to jump into the fray, labelling Corbin's station 'Bogustown' because it wasn't even in the city limits. However, it was far more convenient for potential passengers and shippers than the oxcart access to Mountain Station. 1894 also marked the year Hall Mining began shipping ore direct to Spokane on the N&FS, validating Corbin's claim to his shareholders that the railway would be a success."[7] No longer a dream, the rail link from Nelson to Spokane was complete. The CPR faced another setback in their plan to dominate in the Kootenays.

7   *The Daily Miner (Nelson, BC), March 25, 1895. Courtesy Touch-stones Museum of Art and History, Nelson, BC.*

"Meanwhile, James J. Hill had begun plotting his entry into Canadian Pacific territory. In 1887 he had approached the British Columbia government for a rail charter to run from the US border to Vancouver, connecting to a line he planned to run north from Seattle. Despite opposition from Ottawa, the BC Government granted the charter, and by 1889, construction began on the New Westminster & Southern Railway. On December 2, 1891, the rail lines were complete, and the two trains met: one from Seattle and the other from Canada. The completion of Hill's first venture in Canada predated his main line but indicated his foresight and long-term strategy."[8] This move caused grave concern for Van Horne and the CPR. Their worst nightmare of James J. Hill and the Great Northern in Canada became a reality.

Hill had punched his GN main line to the Pacific coast to completion in 1893, close to the Canadian border across Montana, Idaho and Washington. Hill's vision was to hit CP where it would hurt the most by gaining entry to the Port of Vancouver for the Great Northern. But the New Westminster & Southern Railway was dead-ended on the south bank of the Fraser River. Not only was Hill unable to secure the funding required to build a bridge over the fast-flowing Fraser, 20 miles short of the port, but the CPR had locked in a monopoly on all railway construction north of the Fraser River until 1903. Additionally, the devastating stock market crash of 1893 put the rivalries on hold as the railroads struggled to survive. It would not be until 1904 and the end of the CPR monopoly that a bridge would be constructed over the Fraser, finally allowing

8   Sadis, *The Empire Builder.*

GN access to downtown Vancouver.[9]

But recessions are temporary, and by 1895 the financial markets of North America were improving. The Kootenays were to experience a second boom, and J.J. Hill jumped all over this opportunity. Great Northern Railway had joined the Battle for the Kootenays.

J.J. Hill's next volley came in the mid-1890s when he silently began purchasing stock in Corbin's railways, including the Spokane Falls & Northern and the Nelson & Fort Sheppard, finally taking control in 1898 and removing Daniel Corbin from the company. In addition, Hill and partners had taken over Northern Pacific when it fell into bankruptcy in 1893–94. This purchase provided Great Northern with unchallenged access into the Kootenays from the United States.

Van Horne wasted no time in retaliating. In a surprise move, the CPR bought 100 per cent of John Mara and his partners' CKSN stock and immediately cancelled all steamboat and barge services to Five Mile Point, cutting Hill's access to the mining communities. However, the victory was short-lived. Hill moved swiftly, buying a smaller but competitive steamboat operation, the International Navigation & Trading Company, once again feeding his Nelson & Fort Sheppard Railway with Kootenay ore. Hill would add new and larger vessels to his fleet, bolstering the connection to Spokane.

But perhaps Hill's most daunting move of the 1890s was his decision to finance constructing a narrow-gauge line between Kaslo and Sandon to serve mines extracting quantities

9   *In 2022 Burlington Northern Santa Fe (BNSF) operates freight on this branch line, and Amtrak provides passenger service from Seattle to Vancouver.*

of high-grade silver ore. The charter, issued to BC businessman John Hendry in 1893, never got off the ground. Because of the stock market crash in 1893, Hendry could not secure financing. In early 1895, up stepped Hill, eager to carry the battle to the CPR, and his narrow gauge was the first to reach Sandon in October of 1895.

During the same time frame, Van Horne's Canadian Pacific extended its rail line, the Nakusp & Slocan Railway, east from Nakusp on Arrow Lakes to Sandon. When the CP line arrived in Sandon in December of 1895, the Battle for the Kootenays became ugly.

According to the December 21, 1895, issue of Nelson's *Daily Miner*, in advance of the Nakusp & Sandon line reaching Sandon, the CPR had built a station and freight shed within the townsite. But when the Nakusp & Sandon line was about to enter Sandon on December 15, the battle was on. Led by a battery of lawyers, Hill's superintendent convinced a local magistrate that the CP station was on their land, only metres from the Kaslo & Sandon Railway (K & S) station. The CPR then presented its legal file asserting ownership, convincing a provincial judge to issue a counter-order denying Hill's claim, and CP immediately reclaimed possession.

CP's victory in court enraged Hill, and the next day an order assembled all Kaslo & Sandon Railway crews. Travelling from Kaslo, the 70-plus team arrived in Sandon and demolished the CP station and freight shed in the middle of the night. The CPR telegraph lines were cut, denying any possible assistance. The Kaslo and Slocan employees continued their rampage, pushing the CP employee bunk cars off the tracks and destroying a newly completed trestle on the outskirts of town. By the time CP's help arrived, the Kaslo and Sandon crews had reboarded their train and headed back to Kaslo. Hill denied all accusations that he had ordered the rampage, but it became apparent that he probably had sanctioned the actions over time. Hill's quest for revenge against the CPR continued until his death.

Surprisingly, CP turned the other cheek, acquiescing on its claim to the disputed land, but quickly erected a second station only metres away and repaired the trestle, and the rail line to Nakusp was operational within days. The CP line was standard gauge with fewer physical obstacles and more economical. CP was successfully competing with the K & S.

From the beginning, the terrain and weather, plus substandard construction in the quest to be "first" to reach Sandon, plagued the K & S. While enjoying some early success and profitability into the late 1890s, the line's deficiencies eventually took their toll. Steep grades (3.5 per cent) beyond the accepted railway norms resulted in high operating costs. In winter devastating snow and mudslides often closed the line for weeks at a time. In 1900 Sandon burned to the ground, and labour problems at the mines ended the boom years. It was becoming increasingly difficult to operate profitably.

By 1908 the K & S suspended service to Sandon, needing expensive repairs for slide-damaged bridges and trestles. Then in 1910 a raging forest fire burned bridges and snowsheds, closing the line. In 1911 GN pulled the plug, selling the remnants of the K & S to Kaslo merchants, who revived a portion of the line from Bear Lake to Kaslo. But without the Sandon contracts, the K & S was doomed, and the local owners did not have the capital to repair the Sandon portion. In 1912 the government stepped in, taking over the line, and made the CPR an attractive offer to lease the K & S. CP then rebuilt the line in standard gauge and by 1914 was providing a through rail service from Nakusp to Sandon to Kaslo. Canadian Pacific had wrested control of the West Kootenay back from Hill and the Great Northern.

But the battle was far from over. Rumours of another confrontation in the East Kootenay were rampant. In 1899 a syndicate of investors, apparently headquartered in London, England, announced its intention to build the Bedlington & Nelson Railway from the border to Kuskanook on Kootenay Lake to Hill's Great Northern branch line from Bonners Ferry, Idaho. The new railway would meet the steamboats of the International Navigation & Trading Company from the Kaslo run. It was the worst-kept secret; everyone knew Hill was the money behind the London-based syndicate called the Kootenay Railway and Navigation Company.

Nevertheless, it was a signal loud and clear that Hill would continue the battle for the Kootenays. Van Horne recognized that Hill had to be "cut off at the pass," containing Great Northern where possible at the international boundary. The CPR could no longer procrastinate or play politics; immediate construction of the planned CPR line across southern BC had to commence before Hill could act.

THE BATTLE MOVES EAST:
RAILS TO THE CROWSNEST PASS

By 1895 North American markets had rebounded from the great depression of 1893–94. But Canadian Pacific was still too stretched for capital to consider commencing the second main line through southern British Columbia. Van Horne and the CPR, politically allied with successive Conservative governments, were dubious that the recently elected Liberals, led by Prime Minister Sir Wilfrid Laurier, could be counted on to provide financial assistance to construct the Crowsnest portion of the line. But government money was crucial. Van Horne and his vice-president, Thomas Shaughnessy, approached Clifford Sifton, the Liberal government's Minister of the Interior. Much to their astonishment, Laurier and Sifton showed interest and offered to enter discussions. The CPR eagerly endorsed the offer, entering into formal negotiations to work out a subsidy agreement to allow construction to commence as soon as possible. Next in line was James Baker, who held a charter for his railway dream, the British Columbia Southern Railway. Unable to raise sufficient capital, Baker seized the opportunity to offer his charter to the CPR. Van Horne realized Baker's charter was his footprint to the Pacific, and he accepted his terms.[10]

Surveys began immediately, and despite the political nature of the negotiations, the Crowsnest Agreement resulted,[11] and

10 Sanford, *McCulloch's Wonder*.
11 *The success of the negotiations turned on the offer by Van Horne of a formula of rates to be known as the Crowsnest Agreement and would*

construction began in 1897. Over 300 miles of track were laid in one year in a remarkable effort, much of which was through rugged mountain terrain, driving the last spike of the British Columbia Southern at Kootenay Landing in 1898. CP's elegant sternwheelers (called the "Crow Boats") connected Kootenay Landing with the Nelson railhead and all Kootenay Lake towns and mines. From Nelson, CP trains ran to Trail, Rossland, Midway and Penticton, and in 1916 to Vancouver. Van Horne, no longer playing catch-up, matched Hill and the GN step for step.

Although the rail link from Kootenay Landing to Nelson would have to wait another 30 years, CP continued construction westward on the Columbia & Western Railway from Nelson to Midway. CP had purchased the Columbia & Western from F. Augustus Heinze, and it ran from Rossland to Trail to Castlegar and was chartered to extend to Midway.[12] The terms of the sale for the Columbia & Western included his smelter at Trail, BC, initially unwanted by the CPR. But Heinze held firm, forcing CP to accept the smelter as part of the deal. (It turned out to be an excellent investment. The smelter became far more profitable than the rail venture and grew into a worldwide mining and smelting giant, later known as Columbia Mining & Smelting, currently Teck Resources.) In 1900 spur lines opened

become famous (or infamous) for being the most controversial railway legislation in Canada's history.

12 *The name was suitable for multiple reasons. Midway was halfway between Penticton and Marcus, Washington, at that time its nearest railway point. Midway is near the midpoint on the old Dewdney Trail, from its beginning at Hope to its terminus at Wild Horse Creek near Fort Steele. Midway is also approximately halfway between the Rocky Mountains and the Pacific Ocean. See Britishcolumbia.com.*

to some of the best mines in southern BC, including Kimberley in the Kootenays and Phoenix and Mother Lode copper mines in Boundary Country. For a short while, Canadian Pacific seemed to be on target to dominate British Columbia.

Van Horne and his successor, Thomas Shaughnessy, had long recognized the danger looming on the horizon, even after completing the Crowsnest line to Kootenay Landing and the Columbia & Western to Midway. On November 6, 1898, *The Daily Miner* reported, "In a speech in Winnipeg, in November of 1898, Van Horne foreshadowed the coming struggle when he stated that the Great Northern people would probably be found at the next session of Parliament seeking legislation to build a line into British Columbia; to cut into the trade of that region."[13] Reported the same day, a Spokane paper announced, "The Great Northern is making ready for a great struggle with the Canadian Pacific Railway. The traffic of British Columbia is to be the prize of the battle." On November 7, *The Daily Miner* led with the storyline from the November 5 issue of the *Chicago Tribune*: "Giants Will Battle for The Business." The *Tribune* went on to say, "The Great Northern, it is reported, intends to make application at the next session of the Canadian Parliament to extend the Spokane Falls & Northern through Southern British Columbia."[14]

Indeed, James J. Hill lurked in the background with a surprise agenda. He was well aware of the rich coal fields adjacent to the Crowsnest Pass. In 1897–98 the Crowsnest Pass Coal Company had been incorporated, 100 per cent owned by eastern Canadian

13 *The Daily Miner*, November 6, 1898.
14 *The Daily Miner*, November 7, 1898.

interests.[15] It had attained a lease to 40 miles of coal beds along the Crowsnest route. When CP's Crowsnest line opened in 1898, coal was shipped eastward to fuel CP locomotives, prairie businesses and homes, and the coke was shipped to BC and Montana smelters. The company had built rail lines serving its various collieries, connecting to CP's Crowsnest Railway.

It was then that Hill began to play out his strategy. By 1901 GN had quietly purchased a 30 per cent interest in the Crowsnest Pass Coal Company. Then, very craftily, Hill applied to the British Columbia government to build a rail line entirely in the province, thereby avoiding federal government jurisdiction. Additionally, Hill made it clear he would not require any government subsidies for construction, funding the line independently. That probably swung the deal. Upon approval, Hill immediately began constructing the newly chartered Crowsnest Southern Railway from Morrissey, BC, to the US border. At Morrissey, the Crowsnest Southern connected to a nine-mile spur line to Fernie already owned by the Great Northern Railway through its stake in the Crowsnest Pass

15   The formation of the Crowsnest Pass Coal Company owned by interests other than the CPR was made possible in part by the Crowsnest Agreement between the CPR and the federal government. In return for a generous subsidy grant of $11,000 per mile, the CPR agreed to reduce tariffs for the shipping of western grains eastward and certain industry supplies shipped westward. A most unusual clause was part of the agreement. The CPR agreed to transfer 50,000 acres of coal lands to the federal government that it had received from the BC government as part of the BC Southern Railway charter, to ensure the CPR could not monopolize the coal supply of western Canada. From this clause rose the Crowsnest Pass Coal Company and Hill's eventual "tool of entry" into the fray. See Atlas of Alberta Railways, https://railways.library.ualberta.ca/.

Coal Company.[16]

Construction of the Montana and Great Northern Railway, a branch line from the GN main line at Jennings, Montana, was completed to the border, and in 1902 the lines met. The new rail line began hauling coal and coke south to the United States, advertising three scheduled freights plus one passenger service daily to the GN main line and Spokane.[17] This was a broadside aimed at eroding the success of CP's Crowsnest line, and it hit the mark. By 1905 Hill's railways carried over 70 per cent of the Crowsnest coal and coke volumes south to US markets and the smelters in Grand Forks and fed his main line locomotives high-grade Crowsnest coal. Hill's Crowsnest strategy was a masterstroke and delivered a stunning setback to the CPR.

But nothing lasts forever. At the end of the First World War, the demand for coal that fed the war machine had vanished, and oil began to replace coal as the preferred fuel for steam locomotives. The Spanish flu pandemic devastated an already shattered world, and a hesitant economy stuttered into the 1920s. The demand for Crowsnest coal was declining, and since James J. Hill's death in 1916 the Great Northern's focus on Canada had faded. The Crowsnest Southern Railway had seen better days. The stock market collapse of 1929 and the ensuing Depression sealed its fate. Great Northern abandoned the line, and in the mid-1930s lifted the rails. The bloom had faded from Hill's Kootenay Rose.

16   Canadian Railroad Historical Association, "The Crowsnest Pass,"
Canadian Rail, July–August 1996, 92–93.
17   Canadian Railroad Historical Association, "The Crowsnest Pass," 93.

SHIP AHOY! THE CLASH ON KOOTENAY LAKE

The Battle for the Kootenays was also a struggle to "rule the waves." Kootenay Lake is an inland sea, 104 kilometres long with a 900-kilometre shoreline. This water highway provided access to the wealthiest silver, lead and zinc mines in North America and was ice-free year-round. In 1897, when the CPR bought a controlling interest in the Columbia and Kootenay Steam Navigation Company, Hill responded within weeks, purchasing the International Navigation & Trading Company, operators of two sternwheelers on the lake and river barges on the Kootenay River. The SS *Alberta*, formerly the *State of Idaho*, had been rebuilt for lake service in 1895. The SS *International*, a gracious sternwheeler, was constructed in 1896 to challenge CP's flagship vessel, the SS *Kokanee*.

In early 1898, Great Northern incorporated a new entity, the Kootenay Railway and Navigation Company. The Kaslo & Sandon Railway assets, the soon-to-be-built Bedlington & Nelson Railway, the International Navigation & Trading Company and the planned Kaslo, Lardo and Duncan Railway were folded into the new company.

In 1899 GN's Bedlington & Nelson Railway had been completed from the border to Creston but required a rail connection from Creston Junction to Kuskanook, Kootenay Railway and Navigation's Kootenay Lake landing. The CPR's British Columbia Southern Railway had completed the Crowsnest line from Lethbridge through the Crowsnest Pass to Kootenay Landing in 1898, following the east shore of Kootenay Lake, which effectively blocked any other access to a lakeside landing.

In a rare moment of cooperation, the CPR and the Great Northern reached an agreement to share the CPR line north from Creston Junction, now called Wynndel, to Atbara, a short distance north of Sirdar. Great Northern built a line from Atbara to Kuskanook, the landing for the Kootenay Railway and Navigation sternwheelers. In return, Great Northern allowed the CPR to operate over its track from Nelson (Bogustown) to Five Mile Point. The agreement cleared the way for CP to build from Five Mile to Proctor, providing an ice-free, year-round landing point for the 30-mile steamboat run from Kootenay Landing. The year-round connection to Nelson and the Columbia & Western Railway gave the CPR access to the heart of southern British Columbia. The agreement also allowed GN's Nelson & Fort Sheppard access to downtown Nelson, sharing the new CPR station, opened in 1901, that would offer both CP and GN passenger and freight service.[18]

Having secured the rail connection to Kuskanook, Kootenay Railway and Navigation commissioned the construction of the SS *Kaslo*, the finest steamboat in the Kootenays. "The *Kaslo*" was constructed at Mirror Lake, adjacent to the town of Kaslo, and was built to challenge the CPR's dominance on the lake. Launched in September 1900, she was assigned to the Kaslo, Pilot Bay and Kuskanook routes, transferring cargo and passengers from the Kaslo & Sandon Railway to the Bedlington & Nelson railhead for service to Bonners Ferry and the Great Northern main line, with connections to Spokane. In February of 1900, Kootenay Railway and Navigation launched the *Argenta*, serving the top end of Kootenay Lake and Duncan River.

18   See *Trainweb.org/oldtimetrains/*CPR*/Ships/LandR/Railways.htm.*

Kootenay Railway and Navigation's other sternwheelers, the *International* and the *Alberta*, provided passenger and freight service from Kaslo and Ainsworth to Five Mile Point and Nelson, plus summer excursion charters. In the early 1900s, the expanded Kootenay Railway and Navigation fleet fuelled a fierce rivalry with the CPR boats. By 1902 the company declared its first profit.

But the real nautical presence in the Kootenays belonged to Canadian Pacific. With the purchase of the Columbia and Kootenay Steam Navigation Company, Canadian Pacific had a lock on all navigation on the Columbia River/Arrow Lakes system from Sprott's Landing (Robson) to Revelstoke and dominated Kootenay Lake services. The Columbia River fleet included the *Columbia*, the *Illecillewaet*, the *Lytton*, the *Trail* and the *Nakusp*. On Kootenay Lake, the sternwheelers *Nelson* and *Kokanee*, plus ten barges, controlled most passenger, mail and freight traffic. To meet the challenge of Hill's growing "armada," the SS *Moyie* was commissioned in 1897 and the SS *Kuskanook* in 1906. The largest and most elegantly appointed sternwheeler ever to sail Kootenay Lake, the SS *Nasookin*, was launched in 1913.

Initially a success, by 1906 Kootenay Railway and Navigation experienced financial difficulties, proving a questionable mix of companies, and began the slow slide into insolvency. The company was distanced from the Great Northern at incorporation, hoping overseas investors would snap up all debentures–that was not to happen. GN retained most of the company's debentures to keep it afloat. When the black days came, they struck like a perfect storm, a series of disasters that eventually cost the Great Northern over three million dollars to divest the company.

The first indication of future problems was the failure to gain public support for the passenger service provided by the SS *Kaslo* to Kuskanook, connecting by rail to Spokane. When the CPR completed the route from Lethbridge through the Crowsnest Pass to Kootenay Landing, it became the route of choice for passengers wishing to connect to the outside world. Then a series of marine disasters struck the company. In 1905 the *Alberta* sank near Kaslo, in 1909 the *International*'s boiler gave out and the ship never returned to service. The greatest disaster was the sinking in 1910 of the SS *Kaslo*, blown onto the rocks at Ainsworth. The fleet was lost.

During this timeline, the reality of the Kaslo & Sandon Railway came home to roost. It had been built as a narrow-gauge railway through rocky terrain, and to save construction expenses, the company sacrificed the quality of bridges and the roadbed. The railway's narrow gauge eliminated the ability to barge loaded rail cars across the lake to the Bedlington & Nelson Railway, a standard gauge line. As a result, all ore and cargo had to be offloaded from the Kaslo & Sandon, loaded onto the steamboats, again unloaded and then reloaded onto rail cars. Excessive handling costs made it impossible to compete with the CPR standard gauge lines.

Mother Nature struck the Kaslo & Sandon hard in 1908–10. Consecutive winters of heavy snowfall created avalanches and washouts along the line, interrupting service for months at a time. In 1910 a massive forest fire burned bridges and snowsheds, cutting off the K & S from Sandon and ending passenger and freight service. The K & S made the decision not to rebuild. By 1911 the CPR hauled almost all Sandon ore shipments to Rosebery, then by rail barge across Slocan Lake to CP's railhead at Slocan City. The reassembled train continued to the smelter in Trail.

In 1911 Great Northern liquidated the Kootenay Railway and Navigation Company, selling off the pieces. Local entrepreneurs purchased the K & S, which kept the trains operating to Bear Lake, well short of Sandon. But they were unable to secure the capital to rebuild. By 1914, in a transaction brokered by the government, the CPR took control of the K & S, rebuilding the line to standard gauge and providing service from Kaslo and Sandon to Nakusp. For a few years, the Kootenay Railway and Navigation Company had posed serious competition on Kootenay Lake, but Canadian Pacific had prevailed in the end.

THE BATTLE MOVES WEST: PEACE AT LAST?

When Van Horne retired in 1899, Thomas Shaughnessy became the president of the CPR and would lead the company into the next century. Shaughnessy was Van Horne's protege and, like his mentor, an American, born in Milwaukee in 1853. In 1869, at the age of 16, he joined the Chicago, Milwaukee and St. Paul Railroad. As a store clerk, and over the next few years, his skill with numbers and attention to detail saw him rise quickly through the ranks. In 1880 Shaughnessy was promoted to storekeeper for the company, in charge of all major construction projects, purchases and supplies. In 1882 Van Horne joined the Canadian Pacific Railway as general manager. Construction on the CPR's westward expansion was falling behind schedule, and the financial house was in complete disarray. On his second attempt, Van Horne finally convinced Shaughnessy to leave the United States, offering the purchasing agent position for the entire CPR system. Shaughnessy's tight controls and accounting procedures significantly reduced costs and were instrumental in engineering CP's financial turnaround.[19]

Like Van Horne, Shaughnessy became a rabid supporter of the Canadian Pacific and took out Canadian citizenship. Together, by the time of Van Horne's retirement in 1899, he

19   Theodore D. Regehr, "SHAUGHNESSY, THOMAS GEORGE, 1st Baron SHAUGHNESSY," in Dictionary of Canadian Biography, vol. 15, University of Toronto/Université Laval, 2003–, http://www.biographi.ca/en/bio/ shaughnessy_thomas_george_15E.html.

and Shaughnessy had firmly established the CPR as the premier transportation, shipping and hotel company in North America.

In the early 1900s, a calm had settled on the "battlefields" of British Columbia, and the intense competition between CP and GN had seemingly fizzled out, despite the discovery of vast copper deposits west of the Kootenays in adjacent Boundary County. By 1899 Canadian Pacific had extended the Columbia & Western line to Grand Forks and in 1900 to Midway. That same year the spur line from Eholt summit to the new copper mines commenced operations to the famous Camp Phoenix mine. In May the Granby Consolidated Mining & Smelting Company began shipping ore to CP's smelter at Trail, and later in the year Granby opened a smelter at Grand Forks. CP enjoyed a virtual monopoly in Boundary County for the next three years.

In 1901 James Hill had publicly declared he had no interest in Boundary County. But for Thomas Shaughnessy, Hill's silence was ominous, especially following GN's stunning success in wresting control of the Crowsnest coal mines from the CPR. It was much too quiet.

The silence was shattered in 1902 when Hill once again exploded on the scene, authoring a multi-pronged push into southern British Columbia. Hill's west coast railway charter, the Vancouver, Victoria & Eastern, punched and coerced its way through courts and on the ground, constructing a line from the border to Grand Forks. Hill captured the market with devastating rate cuts.

In 1904 Hill struck again, building a spur line to Phoenix to challenge CP's monopoly: the first ore shipments began in early 1905. Then, taking a page from his Crowsnest coal strategy, Hill purchased a controlling interest in the Granby Consolidated

Mining & Smelting Company, owners of the Phoenix mine, and locked out CP from hauling company ore. Once again, Hill had scuttled CP's dominant position in southern British Columbia.

Challenging CP's stranglehold on the Port of Vancouver, Hill's New Westminster & Southern finally bridged the Fraser River and laid track into the heart of the city, accessing the docks. But Hill was not yet satisfied with his assault on CP and announced in late 1904 that he was ready to build his third main line following the Kettle River into Canada, surveying a right-of-way through the Cascade Mountains to Vancouver.

When confronting Hill and the Great Northern's expansion into Canada, Van Horne's policy had been to apply maximum political pressure and, when all else failed, raise the flag of Canadian nationalism. For years these strategies had proven successful, but the economic landscape of North America was changing. Political processes alone were no longer enough to win the day. Shaughnessy decided to tackle Hill in his backyard in a bold new direction for the CPR. Hence came another twist in the "tangled web" that provided Canadian Pacific with a golden opportunity to strike back and deliver a smashing blow to GN's northwest monopoly.

Daniel Corbin, ousted by Hill in 1897 when Great Northern took control of his railways, reappeared on the Kootenay scene. He was more than eager to strike back at Hill for "stealing" his companies and saw an opportunity to settle an old score. In 1905 he announced plans to build a rail line from Spokane to the border at Eastport, Idaho, and Kingsgate, British Columbia, that would connect to the CPR's Crowsnest line, engaging the Great Northern on home turf. But this time the Canadian Pacific, Corbin's former foe, had become a formidable ally. The CPR was ready and willing to have a go at Hill and provided Corbin's financing required for construction. In 1906 Corbin's Spokane International Railway had reached the border at Eastport, Idaho, and was connected to the CPR's Crowsnest line by an eight-mile spur to Yahk, BC.

Thomas Shaughnessy left little doubt he meant to do business in the United States. Six deluxe passenger train sets, delivered to the Soo Line, CP's American subsidiary, commenced a first class express service, Saint Paul and Minneapolis to Spokane. The Soo-Spokane Train Deluxe attacked Hill in his heartland, breaking the Spokane monopoly. In a later agreement with the Oregon Railway & Navigation Line (part of the Union Pacific network), the route extended to Portland, Oregon, renamed the Soo-Spokane-Portland Train Deluxe. By a quirk of geography, the Soo-CP-Spokane International route was shorter than the Great Northern or Northern Pacific main lines, resulting in a faster timetable and a competitive edge.

Additionally, the quality and luxury of the train sets were unmatched in the day, and over the next year the US government cancelled GN's contract for mail between Minneapolis/Saint Paul to Spokane and the northwest, awarding it to the CPR. With a virtual slap across the face, Van Horne and Shaughnessy had dealt Hill and the Great Northern a stunning blow.

Losing the US mail contract to the CPR drove Hill over the top; he vowed instant revenge, livid and enraged beyond belief. In late spring of 1907, he announced plans to add a third main line to the GN system, from Spokane into southern BC and through to Vancouver. The survey work would commence immediately for a rail line from Fernie, his terminus in the Crowsnest, to Calgary and beyond to Grand Prairie in northern Alberta, plus another line to Medicine Hat and Winnipeg. Hill boasted that Canada would have a second transcontinental railway.[20] The skirmish that had begun in Sandon in 1895 had escalated into a full-scale war.

In April of 1907, Hill's son, Louis, succeeded him as president and endorsed his father's plans for the rail line to Vancouver. Hill remained as chairman, still maintaining a grip over the board of directors, some of whom were beginning to question the profitability of GN's increasingly aggressive expansion into British Columbia, but to no avail.

In late 1907, the economy plunged into a depression. Railway expansion was put on hold or cancelled. The promise of a rail line across southern British Columbia by either Great Northern or the CPR began to look elusive.

By 1909 the economic climate had improved, and the race was back on. The final piece of the puzzle was the right-of-way through the Coquihalla to Hope. Whoever controlled the right-of-way would win this battle by acclamation, as there was hardly room for one rail line through the canyon, let alone two.

By 1911 the Great Northern's board of directors openly questioned Hill's priority for funding the Canadian route through the Coquihalla to Vancouver. The expansion into British Columbia no longer enjoyed unquestioned support. But Hill's vision of a north–south axis was still intact; he was an ardent free trader. He recognized the benefits to Great Northern if there were no tariffs and duties between the two countries. And in Canada he found an unlikely ally.

Wilfrid Laurier, the leader of the Liberal Party, had been elected prime minister of Canada in 1896 and went on to win four successive elections. Laurier was a wily politician and had long sensed that a trade and tariff agreement with the United

---

20   Sanford, *McCulloch's Wonder.*

States was necessary. By the early 1900s, trade relations with the us became a dominant issue, and Laurier became the champion of reciprocity. After years of discussions and negotiations, in 1911 Laurier's Finance Minister William Steves Fielding announced a free trade reciprocity agreement ratified by the us government. So assured of widespread support across Canada, Laurier called an election to endorse his trade policy. Laurier's re-election looked like a foregone conclusion.[21]

But a funny thing happened on the way to the polls. Out of the ashes of retirement, an old but familiar warrior arose, none other than William Cornelius Van Horne, to join the Conservatives to fight against the free traders. Although an American by birth, Van Horne's loyalty to Canada and the CPR rose to the forefront. He boldly confronted his opposition, declaring reciprocity would kill "Canada's Company," the CPR. The Conservatives contended that reciprocity was the first step to American annexation.

In a landslide, Laurier suffered a humiliating defeat. The old warrior had brandished his sword and struck a devastating blow. The demise of reciprocity ended Hill's dream of goods flowing duty-free across the border and final victory over the CPR. The defeat also marked the beginning of the end for the unwavering support for Hill from senior business managers and the GN board of directors. The political clout of the CPR in Canada was still unchallenged.[22]

21 *Real Belanger, "LAURIER, SIR WILFRID," in Dictionary of Canadian Biography, vol. 14, University of Toronto/Université Laval, 2003–, http://www.biographi.ca/en/theme_laurier.html?p=1.*
22 *It would take 83 years (1994) before the North American Free Trade Agreement would be signed into law between the United States and Canada.*

Despite the defeat of reciprocity, the quest for the right-of-way through the Coquihalla continued. Even when the board of railway commissioners had suggested "that it would be an incredible achievement to build even one railway through the Coquihalla Pass, let alone two," both railways seemingly ignored the report.[23] But abruptly, in the fall of 1912, construction on both lines halted. External communication from the railways ground to a halt.

Then came an announcement that stunned British Columbians and the railway industry at large. L.C. Gilman, assistant to the president of GN, offered to abandon any claim to the lower Coquihalla canyon. Great Northern agreed that the Kettle Valley Railway could build the Coquihalla line if the Vancouver, Victoria & Eastern could lease trackage rights at a reasonable fee. Like a bolt out of the blue, the management at Great Northern completely reversed its position. On April 9, 1913, the Kettle Valley Railway began construction on the final leg through the canyon to Hope.[24]

On July 31, 1916, British Columbia's long-sought southern main line opened for rail traffic, and CP's Kettle Valley Railway commenced passenger service to Vancouver. For almost 30 years, the two railways had see-sawed from victory to defeat and back again. Finally, the battle was over, and the Canadian Pacific Railway had prevailed.

23 *Sanford, McCulloch's Wonder, 158–159.*
24 *Sanford, McCulloch's Wonder, 158–159.*

PART II
The Trains to Gold and Silver

NELSON BECOMES THE HUB

The CPR built the first train station in Nelson in 1891. It was a single-story warehouse-style structure with the telegraph operator and ticket office, built as the Columbia & Kootenay Railway terminus. It was a short journey to Sproat's Landing (near present-day Castlegar), providing connections to the CPR main line in Revelstoke via sternwheelers on Arrow Lakes.

Then, in the late fall of 1893, Daniel Corbin's Nelson & Fort Sheppard Railway breached the top of the Cottonwood Pass, with plans to follow the grade down to the Nelson townsite. But that was not to be. British Columbia's Premier Robson had previously granted the Canadian Pacific the exclusive rights to all foreshore surrounding Nelson. But Corbin never missed a beat. He continued building above and beyond the CPR's rights to Five Mile Point on the west arm of Kootenay Lake, constructing a terminal and pier, servicing the lake's sternwheelers and barges.

But Corbin needed a Nelson terminal to cash in on the lucrative passenger traffic predicted for his Spokane connection. Choosing a site above the town and beyond any rights or claims of the CPR, he constructed Mountain Station, with a wagon road connection into Nelson. He had slipped out of the CPR's gambit to contain his access to Nelson and Kootenay Lake. Now the city could claim a second railway station, with service to the Spokane main lines of the Great Northern and Northern Pacific railways. Connections were now available to all points in the United States.

In 1898 the CPR completed the Crowsnest Railway to Kootenay Landing. CP's sternwheelers met the trains and transported passengers and freight across the lake to Nelson. As passenger volumes increased and westward traffic to the copper discoveries in Boundary County grew exponentially, the CPR proposed that Nelson become a divisional point that required expanding the existing rail yard, construction of maintenance and repair shops, a new station and another wharf. In a community referendum on December 6, 1899, the council passed a bylaw supporting the CP proposal.[25] In September of 1899, construction began on the station and shops. On January 1, 1901, the *Nelson Tribune* reported, "The new Union Passenger Depot went into service this morning." On January 4, 1901, the headline read, "The Nelson and Fort Sheppard business will also be transacted from the new freight depot alongside the CPR clerks."

In 1898 Hill and the Great Northern assumed ownership of the Nelson & Fort Sheppard Railway. The CPR's greatest menace was "in town." But the CPR and the Great Northern had a common need, which resulted in the agreement to share CP's Nelson station. The CPR required access to the GN tracks from Nelson to Five Mile Point. From there, a rail link to Procter would allow an ice-free landing on Kootenay Lake. Similarly, Great Northern required rail access on the CPR line from Creston to Sirdar to complete the Bedlington & Nelson Railway from Bonner's Ferry to Kuskanook, the landing for Kootenay Railway and Navigation Company sternwheelers.

25   On December 6, 1899, Bylaw 57 passed by a large majority in a vote by city taxpayers and was passed and adopted by council. *The Tribune (Nelson, BC), December 7, 1899.*

This agreement would prove to be an anomaly, but through 1901 it was all quiet on the BC front.

In February, with the new sheds and warehouse buildings erected, construction focused on the waterfront, and by the spring of 1901 the new dock was in place.[26] Nelson emerged as the central hub on the proposed southern main line across southern British Columbia.

In the early 1900s, Nelson was the third-largest city in British Columbia. When incorporated in 1897, the population was 3,000 residents, and by 1910 it was a bustling city of over 8,000. In 1899 Nelson boasted an electric utility company, a gasworks plant and an electrified streetcar system. Canadian Pacific's decision to establish its regional headquarters in Nelson secured the city's prosperity into the 1950s. Sandon, Ainsworth, Riondel, Kaslo, New Denver, Silverton and Slocan City were booming, and the future was rosy.

Daily transcontinental service on the Canadian Pacific southern main line and passenger service via the Great Northern to Spokane, Washington, passed through the Nelson station, as did the local trains to the surrounding mines, towns and villages. Seamless schedules connected the trains to the sternwheelers plying the waters of Kootenay Lake, accessing the lakeshore communities. All rolling stock was serviced or repaired in CP's maintenance shop. The shipyards, another CPR division, constructed and maintained the sternwheelers on the lake. In 1910 Nelson was "the place to be" in British Columbia.

26 *The Tribune, 1901. Newspaper files courtesy Touchstones Museum of Art and History, Nelson.*

THE TRAINS OF THE KOOTENAYS

In 2010 ownership of the train station passed from the CPR to the Nelson Chamber of Commerce. For the citizens, it was a wish come true. CP had neglected the station for years, and it was in a state of near collapse, with rotten timbers, roof leaks and mould. Thankfully, through community support, donors and government grants, this classic station has been lovingly restored. A refurbished waiting room and ticket office area contain a tasteful information centre and cafe, and in front of the building two '50s-era diesel locomotives are on display. But the restoration, while an outstanding accomplishment, offers scant information chronicling the principal role the station had played in the community and even less evidence regarding the sophisticated passenger train and steamboat connections that once served all of the Kootenays. More and better public transportation was available to residents 120 years ago than today.

Nelson was the nerve centre, and the railways were the foremost employers during the heyday of train travel. Everything that arrived or departed, including the travellers, immigrants, tourists, executives, foodstuffs, merchandise, heavy-duty equipment and cars of coal and ore, went through this station, with connections branching out to all surrounding mines and communities.

In 1891 there was only one train a day from Nelson to Sproat's Landing. The train connected to Columbia and Kootenay Steam Navigation's steamboat service on the Columbia River to Trail Creek and Northport, Washington. The Arrow Lakes service to the CPR main line at Revelstoke, BC, was the other connection. But by 1899, with the completion of the Crowsnest Line to Kootenay Landing, Nelson was suddenly connected by daily train service to the rest of Canada and the United States. Daily Canadian Pacific departures from Montreal, Toronto and points east were available to Nelson, requiring only a seamless connection in Medicine Hat. International bankers travelled the route, as did investors, early tourists and scoundrels, all headed to the boom towns of western Canada's exploding mining activity. The Kootenays had become a magnet for the committed and curious, eager to participate in the coming "bonanza." The world was banging on the Kootenay door.

THE CANADIAN PACIFIC NETWORK

By 1907 CP's passenger travel was flourishing. CPR's first transcontinental trains were the westbound Pacific Express and the eastbound Atlantic Express.[27] The Pacific Express from Montreal and Toronto connected with Train 5, eventually named the Kootenay Express, at Dunmore, Alberta, the late evening of the third night. It was a slick connection, departing minutes later, crossing Alberta's southern prairies to Lethbridge, Fort Macleod and Pincher Creek. The train entered the Rockies in the early morning, crossing the Continental Divide via the Crowsnest Pass. The train arrived at Kootenay Landing on the south end of Kootenay Lake midafternoon on day four. Passengers would disembark and board the SS *Moyie*, CPR's

27   *All schedule and timetable information courtesy Steve Boyko, www. traingeek.ca, the Rossland Museum & Discovery Centre, Trail Library and Archives and Touchstones Museum of Art and History in Nelson, BC.*

Crow Boat. Now on display in Kaslo, the gracious sternwheeler boasted 13 staterooms and a deluxe dining room with a capacity of over 350 passengers. A four-hour sailing landed the *Moyie* in Nelson in the early evening.

The Atlantic Express, Train 6 eastbound from Vancouver, offered Nelson and the Kootenays similar connections. Departing Vancouver daily at 3:30 pm, an overnight journey arrived in Revelstoke at 8:30 am. Nelson passengers transferred to Train 22 for Arrowhead, arriving at 10:00 am, and then boarded the awaiting SS *Minto*, sister ship to the SS *Moyie*, sailing at 10:15 am. An all-day journey on Arrow Lakes arrived in Robson at 8:00 pm, with connections to the Columbia & Western Train 10 at 8:45 pm to Nelson, arriving at 10:15 pm. The surprising network of CP trains and steamboats operated on time, barring interference from Mother Nature.

Both transcontinental trains operated similar equipment, catering to all levels of passengers. Standard equipment on Train 95, the Pacific Express, out of Montreal, included a baggage/mail car, a first class coach, first class sleeping car, a Colonist car and tourist sleepers on Tuesday, Wednesday, Friday and Saturday, plus a through sleeper from Boston on Tuesdays. On Mondays and Thursdays, tourist sleepers from Toronto were added. Extra sleeping cars were available as needed in Winnipeg.

Train 96, the Atlantic Express, eastbound from Vancouver, had identical equipment. Tourist sleepers for Boston ran on Wednesday, Montreal on Tuesday, Wednesday, Friday and Saturday and Toronto Monday, Wednesday and Thursday. The train also ran a first class sleeper and a tourist sleeper to Saint Paul via the Soo Line connection in Moose Jaw.

Train 5, from Medicine Hat to Kootenay Landing, offered a shorter consist including one first class and one second class coach, a first class sleeper and a cafe car. The head-end "working" cars could include at least one Dominion Express car in addition to the baggage car to meet the growing demand for merchandise in the new, booming communities. Train 6 returned to Medicine Hat with an identical consist.

Passengers proceeding beyond Nelson could find a connection to almost anywhere in the West Kootenay, either by rail or a Canadian Pacific or a Kootenay Railway and Navigation (Great Northern) sternwheeler. Trains to Trail, Robson, Castlegar and Rossland departed twice daily. CP's Columbia & Western Train 9 also offered daily service to Castlegar, Robson, Grand Forks, Eholt Junction or Midway, with connections to the mining community of Phoenix.

Nelson Landing, adjacent to the station, was every bit as active. The CP and GN sternwheelers carried passengers and cargo to all points on Kootenay Lake, including Kootenay Landing, Gray Creek, Ainsworth, Riondel, Kaslo, Lardeau, Duncan and Argenta, with intermediate flag stops at smaller communities en route. Train connections to Slocan City were met by the CP sternwheeler SS *Slocan*, across Slocan Lake to Rosebery, then boarding the Sandon–Nakusp train. The SS *Minto* met Robson's train connections for service up Arrow Lakes to Nakusp and Arrowhead, then by rail to Revelstoke. It was an ingenious network.

THE GREAT NORTHERN NETWORK

Similarly, GN's Nelson & Fort Sheppard Railway offered daily service from Nelson to Spokane, with connections from Sandon and Kaslo via the Kaslo & Sandon Railway and GN's fleet of sternwheelers. In Spokane, travellers could connect to the Great Northern or Northern Pacific main lines with daily service eastbound to Minneapolis/Saint Paul and connections to Chicago and New York. Daily service westbound served Seattle and Portland, with links to San Francisco.

In 1905 Great Northern introduced its all-new train between Saint Paul and Puget Sound, called the Oriental Limited. The *Railway and Engineering Review* of November 11, 1905, included the following announcement: "On November 19, the Great Northern Railway will start a new (and additional) train between St. Paul and Puget Sound Points. This will be known as the Oriental Limited and will have new car equipment throughout."

The Oriental Limited consisted of the latest equipment and was hailed as the "perfect train." The lead car was an RPO (railway post office), followed by the baggage and express car. A 71-seat second class coach and an 81-passenger first class coach, positioned ahead of two tourist sleepers, were followed by a 30-seat dining car. A first class Palace sleeper and tail-end observation car, with one drawing room, four compartments, a card room, a small buffet and a 15-seat observation room, completed the consist. Ornately decorated, they were the first of their kind to be used in transcontinental service.[28] Canadian Pacific faced stiff competition for long-haul passengers.

But it didn't take the CPR long to meet the challenge. As previously detailed, in 1907 Thomas Shaughnessy announced the Soo-Spokane Train Deluxe from Minneapolis and Saint Paul through the Crowsnest Pass to Spokane, Washington. From Nelson, heading to the Midwest or the eastern seaboard, eastbound passengers could connect to the Soo-Spokane at

28   For more on the Oriental Limited, see https://www.gnflyer. com/1905oL.html.

Cranbrook and connect on arrival in Saint Paul for service to Chicago.[29]

Launched initially as a seasonal service, the Soo-Spokane Train Deluxe was an immediate success. Within months, CPR/Soo Line management announced that the train would operate daily on a year-round schedule. In 1908, in agreement with the Oregon Railway & Navigation Line (a Union Pacific Company and another nemesis of J.J. Hill's), the route was extended to Portland, Oregon, and rebranded the Soo-Spokane Portland Train Deluxe. The CPR had stunned the railway world with the success of its bold gamble, cracking Great Northern's supposedly unassailable monopoly in the northwest.

THE SOO-SPOKANE TRAIN DELUXE

In 1907 Barney & Smith Company delivered an order for six complete train sets, launching an all new international service titled the Soo-Spokane Train Deluxe, a joint venture of the Canadian Pacific Railway and its US subsidiary, the Soo Line. This deluxe train linked the Twin Cities of Minneapolis and Saint Paul with Spokane, Washington, the heart of the Inland Empire, with an interesting twist–the service travelled through western Canada instead of the Midwestern states. Remarkably, the route was ten miles shorter than the GN main line and 40 miles less than the Northern Pacific main line. The train was more than competitive and recognized as the premier passenger train in North America and the first train in North America with electric lighting throughout.

29   *All Soo Line schedules and information courtesy Soo Line Historical and Technical Society, Appleton, Wisconsin.*

The tail-end cars were a wonder of craftsmanship and design. Beautifully proportioned and luxuriously outfitted, they graced the end of each train with their brass-railed open platforms, electrically lit domes and coloured striped canopies. Each car's rear end had a new feature: an electrically illuminated circular tailboard sign spelling out "Soo-Spokane Train Deluxe."

In each train set, ahead of the tail-end observation car with a library, buffet and four compartments, was a 12-section, one first class compartment sleeper, followed by the dining car, the first class coach, the tourist sleeper, and the head end, the mail express baggage car. Leading the consist was a fast and powerful Pacific-type locomotive, capable of maintaining a high-speed schedule. Overall, 36 rail cars were built exclusively for this service, providing the six train sets required to operate a daily service.[30]

The trains were numbered and named. Train 151, the Soo-Spokane-Portland Train Deluxe, departed the Twin Cities of Minneapolis/Saint Paul daily at 10:00 pm. A Sunday departure would have you arrive in Cranbrook at 3:05 pm on Tuesday, Spokane that same evening at 8:00 pm and Portland at 11:00 am Wednesday. Train 150, the eastbound Soo-Spokane-Portland Train Deluxe, departed Portland daily at 9:00 pm. A Sunday departure had you in Spokane at 3:00 pm Monday, Cranbrook at 10:30 pm and the Twin Cities at 4:55 pm on Wednesday. In addition to the surging ridership from Chicago, Saint Paul and Minneapolis, the "local" market from Cranbrook and the Crowsnest mining communities eagerly welcomed this classy and convenient train to Spokane. For years Canadians had

30   *Information about the Soo-Spokane Train Deluxe courtesy Cranbrook History Centre.*

been hungering for access to the variety of better and cheaper goods in the United States, and now it was only a day trip away. Demand was beyond all expectations. The CPR had a winner.

In just a few short years, the Kootenays had become the mining and industrial capital of the province and second only to Vancouver as a financial centre. The trains connected the Kootenays to the world, and the stations had become the busiest places in town.

A DAY AT THE STATION

To spend a day at the Nelson depot and adjacent CP wharf in the early 1900s would be a rail buff's dream come true. With the commencement of passenger rail service on the Crowsnest line to Kootenay Landing and the agreement between the CPR and the Great Northern in 1901 to share the new station, it became a whirlwind of activity from early morning into the late evening.

To pick a year, a typical day in 1906 began around 5:00 am as local business owners and cartage haulers arrived at the freight shed to claim their shipments of merchandise, hardware, tools and construction supplies, or food and perishables for delivery to local and regional stores and restaurants. The trains that arrived the previous evening brought goods from Spokane on GN's Nelson & Fort Sheppard Railway and from across Canada on the CP rail and steamer connections from the main line at Revelstoke. At the same time, passengers began to arrive at the station, checking in for the 6:30 am departure for Kootenay Landing on the SS *Kuskanook*, the assigned Crow Boat for the four-hour Kootenay Landing sailing. Passengers then boarded Train 5, eastbound for Creston, Moyie, Cranbrook, Fernie, Fort Macleod, Calgary, Lethbridge or Medicine Hat, for connections to main line services.[31]

---

31   *Train and steamboat schedules and information courtesy Steve Boyko, www.traingeek.ca, the Rossland Museum & Discovery Centre, the Trail Museum and Archives, Touchstones Museum of Art and History in Nelson and the Kootenay Lake Archives in Kaslo.*

Even before the *Kuskanook* left the dock, boarding commenced for Train 9, the daily service to Castlegar, Robson West (connections to Trail and Rossland), Grand Forks, Eholt and Midway, departing 7:15 am. At 8:10, the train to Slocan City eased into the platform to load, leaving at 8:25. On arrival at Slocan City, ongoing passengers boarded the SS *Slocan* to Rosebery, with rail connections east to Sandon or north to Nakusp. Passengers proceeding past Nakusp boarded the SS *Minto*, sailing to Halcyon Hot Springs and Arrowhead, where an awaiting train boarded the passengers for Revelstoke and points on the CPR main line. As soon as the Slocan service departed, the Nelson & Fort Sheppard's Train 261 to Spokane commenced boarding for a 9:05 am departure for Five Mile, Mountain, Salmo and Beaver Falls before crossing the border. At Northport, Washington, Rossland passengers from the Red Mountain Railway connected. Arrival in Spokane was 5:45 pm.

Following the Spokane departure, busy inbound arrivals began with back-to-back steamers. At 10:25, GN's SS *International* arrived from Kaslo, Ainsworth, Balfour and intermediate points, closely followed by the CP steamer from Gray Creek, Crawford Bay and Procter at 10:30 and the SS *Moyie* from Kaslo at 11:00 am. Sandwiched between the steamer arrivals was the train from Rossland, Trail and Castlegar at 10:50 pm.

A welcomed lull followed the hectic morning arrivals and departures, but traffic through the station remained brisk. The adjoining express and freight building housed both the CPR and the Great Northern agents accepting or delivering consignments, and the baggage check-in and storage was open all day. The coffee shop and newsstand bustled throughout the day, and the telegraph office had a steady stream of businessmen and individuals communicating their messages to the outside world.

Around 2:00 pm, the next surge of passengers would arrive, preparing to board the 3:00 pm sailing of the CP steamer to Procter, Crawford Bay and Gray Creek, or the train at 3:15 for Castlegar, Trail and Rossland. At 4:00 pm, CP's SS *Moyie* departed, followed by the SS *International* at 4:30, sailing for Kaslo. The *International* would meet Nelson & Fort Sheppard Train 262 from Spokane at Five Mile Point, taking passengers for Kaslo and intermediate points. After the Five Mile meet, Train 262 continued to Nelson, arriving at 5:20 pm.

But the station's day was far from over. The next wave descended for the 6:40 departure to Castlegar, Trail and Rossland. It was often one of the busiest trains because it also carried passengers connecting to the SS *Minto* for the overnight sailing to Revelstoke and the CP main line. Then, at 8:00 pm, the Crow Boat, the SS *Kuskanook*, returned from Kootenay Landing with passengers from Train 5, later named the Kootenay Express. This arrival carried up to 200-plus passengers, filling the Nelson hotels. The following day, many would have had connections to Trail, Rossland, Kaslo and Midway, feeding the CP network.

The last arrival of the day was Train 10 from Midway, arriving at 10:15 pm, often a full house, carrying passengers from the mines and smelters in Phoenix and Grand Forks and passengers from Rossland and Trail who boarded at Castlegar. Additional Nelson passengers boarded in Robson West who would have disembarked from the SS *Minto* or the SS *Rossland* from Revelstoke.

Michael Cone, author, freelance writer and pre-eminent authority on the history of Kootenay Lake sternwheelers, explained the seamless procedures employed in Nelson that connected train passengers to the steamboats: "The westbound train would have backed down to the dock before the Crow

Boat's arrival. The stewards handled passenger luggage. Once the westbound train was loaded and had departed, the east-bound train would arrive at the dock. Passengers transferred from the train to the boat, taking a stateroom for the night to make a painless 6:30 am departure for Kootenay Landing. Local passengers could do one of two things: they could book a state-room and board the boat the night before departure, or board in the early morning commencing one hour before departure. Finally, the station was quiet for a few hours while everyone caught their breath for a repeat performance the next day."

Up the lake in Kaslo, a similar performance played out. Kaslo was a Great Northern town, the main terminus of the Kaslo & Sandon Railway, the home port of GN's sternwheeler fleet and the heart of the Kootenay mining boom. Nearby, Mirror Lake housed the shipyard. In the early 1900s, it was a well-established community of over 5,000 residents, and a day at the station would have been an illuminating experience. Rich ore deposits on Kaslo Creek brought in prospectors by the hundreds. In 1894 the pop-ulation had exploded to over 3,000 souls. In a high narrow valley 30 miles to the west, the town of Sandon experienced another mining boom, and by 1900 boasted a population of 5,000. The Kaslo and Sandon railway, completed to Sandon in 1895, trans-ported the ore to the docks at Kaslo, and it was then loaded onto barges and steamboats, shipped to the Nelson & Fort Sheppard railhead at Five Mile Point and from there delivered to the hun-gry smelters in Northport and Spokane, Washington.

In the late 1890s, ore discoveries at the top end of Kootenay Lake added to the frenzy. In addition to shipping volumes of ore, hundreds of people, tons of merchandise, mining equip-ment, foodstuffs and staples required transportation. Both the CPR and the Great Northern responded with steamboat service. Kaslo became the "mother ship," with connections to all communities on the lake. The banner on the front page of the *Kootenaian*, the daily newspaper, said it best: "Kaslo Is the Only Town From Which Every Mining Camp In Kootenay Can Be Reached In One Day."

The day started early on the docks and at the adjacent train station. Hundreds of bags of ore had been unloaded off the Kaslo & Sandon train the night before from the Sandon, Big Bear and Whitewater mines. By 5:00 am, the wharfies were hard at work, loading the ore into the belly of Kootenay Railway and Navigation's SS *International*. The ship's stewards assisted passengers with luggage, preparing for departure to Ainsworth, Pilot Bay, Balfour, Five Mile Point and Nelson at 6:00 am. Ore was offloaded at the smelter in Pilot Bay before a close connection was made with the Nelson & Fort Sheppard Railway at Five Mile Point for the train to Spokane.

Meanwhile, back in Kaslo, the *International* would have barely cleared the bay when CP's SS *Moyie* commenced boarding for a 7:00 am departure to Nelson from the CPR wharf. The two companies were bitter rivals on the lake, operating competing services in a fierce battle of attrition.

Next up was the SS *Kaslo*, the flagship of Kootenay Railway and Navigation's fleet and an 8:00 am departure. The *Kaslo* was launched in 1901 and immediately assigned the new route to Kuskanook Landing, connecting to the Bedlington, Nelson and Kootenai Railway with service to Bonners Ferry in the United States and the Great Northern main line. At 8:00 am, the Kaslo & Sandon train departed for South Fork, Whitewater, Bear Lake and Sandon. The SS *Argenta* eased into the dock at 9:30, loading for the Monday, Wednesday and Friday departures to Lardeau, Argenta and Duncan River camps.

CP and GN freighters and barges sailed out of Kaslo and Nelson throughout the day, transporting equipment, merchandise, dry goods and food supplies to communities around the lake. Most of the freighters accepted passengers but did not run on posted schedules. When they had a load, they were on their way. There was no lack of public transportation in 1906!

The late afternoon was usually the busiest time of the day. At 3:50 pm, the K & S arrived from Sandon with two coaches and boxcars filled with ore and unloaded at the dock. The SS *Kokanee* boarded passengers and cargo at the CPR wharf for the 4:30 pm departure to Lardeau, with Gerrard and Trout Lake City connections.[32]

At 5:10 pm, the *Argenta* returned to Kaslo from the North Kootenay run. Another breather lasted until 8:00 pm and the busiest arrivals of the day, both from Nelson. First in was the SS *Moyie*, followed by the SS *International* at 8:30. A typical day drew to a close at 10:00 pm with the return of the SS *Kokanee* from Lardeau.

32   Lardeau arrival was 8:00 pm and ongoing passengers boarded a mixed train that arrived in Gerrard at 9:45 pm. At 10:00 pm a connecting steamboat, the SS Victoria, sailed to the final destination of Trout Lake City, arriving at midnight.

TRAINS TO ROSSLAND AND TRAIL

Another railway boom was on at the south end of the Kootenays as competing railways scrambled to reach Rossland and Trail. In the early 1890s, the new claims staked in the Rossland area had shifted the focus of the mining interests from Nelson to Red Mountain. "There's gold in them thar hills!" was the cry, and indeed there was! The core of Red Mountain was the cone of an extinct volcano, laced with rich veins of gold and copper ore. The word was out; a "Golden City" had been discovered. By the time the mines began to peter out in the 1920s, over 80 tonnes of gold, representing over three billion dollars at today's prices, was mined.

In 1895 a brash young entrepreneur followed the gold rush to Rossland. At 26 years of age, Fritz Augustus Heinze was one of Butte, Montana's "Copper Kings." In August of that year, he announced he would build a smelter on the Columbia River at Trail Creek Landing to treat the gold and copper ore, intercepting the ore from Rossland mines headed to smelters south of the border. He was fully aware he'd need a conveyance to transport the ore from the mines to his smelter, and he set out to build both.

After announcing his smelter, Heinze contracted for ore from the Le Roi mine and began construction. The smelter was blown-in in June of 1896. Concurrent with the construction of the smelter, Heinze built his narrow-gauge railway, called the Columbia & Western, to Rossland, driving the last spike at the Le Roi mine, also in June of 1896. On June 11, the first trainload of ore left the mine for Heinze's smelter, and passenger service commenced the same day.

Daniel Corbin was hard on his heels, building a branch line from Northport, Washington, connecting his Spokane Falls & Northern Railway to the mines at Rossland. Corbin's master plan included a smelter at Northport to compete with Heinze's Trail Creek operation. Corbin began construction in 1895, hoping to be Rossland's first railway, but halted at the edge of the Colville Indian Reserve. Corbin required congressional approval to build through the reserve. In March of 1896, President Grover Cleveland eventually signed the legislation that allowed his Columbia and Red Mountain Railway to proceed. Corbin finally reached Rossland in December of 1896, six months behind Heinze's Columbia & Western. Corbin's first passenger train to Spokane departed Rossland on December 19. Rossland could now boast two railways serving the mines and passenger service connecting to the outside world. By 1897 both Rossland and Trail could boast populations exceeding 5,000 residents, and the boom was in full swing.[33]

In 1897 Rossland's access to the outside world continued to grow as Heinze expanded the footprint of the Columbia & Western Railway, constructing a standard gauge line from Trail Creek to West Robson. Heinze now had access to the Canadian Pacific steamboats on Arrow Lakes to Revelstoke and the CP main line and connections to CP's Columbia & Kootenay Railway to Nelson. Heinze's charter also included the authority to build from Rossland to the Okanagan, and this was the plum

---

33   J.D. McDonald, *The Railways of Rossland and British Columbia* (Trail, BC: Hall Printing, 1991). *Courtesy Rossland Museum & Discovery Centre.*

that led to CP's bid to purchase Heinze's Columbia & Western. The Crowsnest Pass line was due for completion to Nelson in 1898. Canadian Pacific was determined to extend its rail line into Boundary County, heading off possible American railway incursions into the developing copper mines of Boundary Country. CP first offered to buy only the Columbia & Western Railway and charter, but Heinze declined the offer, demanding that the condition of sale include his Trail Creek smelter. At the time, Canadian Pacific had little interest in a smelter and backed away. But Heinze knew the charter was his ace in the hole and held out, calling CP's bluff. In the end, CP agreed to the total package. The irony of the deal was that the smelter would turn into CP's crown jewel in the Kootenays.

The year 1898 proved to be a milestone for the railways. The Crowsnest Pass route was completed from the CP main line at Medicine Hat to Kootenay Landing with a seamless connection to Nelson by CP's steamboat services. Rossland and Trail were now accessible by rail from all across Canada, including the banking and stock exchange centres of Montreal, Toronto, Winnipeg, Calgary and Vancouver.

But an equally important series of events had played out that same year in the stock exchanges across the United States. An unknown entity was stealthily buying up shares in Corbin's railways, eventually purchasing controlling interest. When the smoke cleared, J.J. Hill and his Great Northern Railway emerged as owners of the Spokane Falls & Northern and the Nelson & Fort Sheppard railways. Corbin was out. But the good news for Rossland, Trail and the Kootenays were the lower freight rates resulting from the increased competition, as Canadian Pacific and Great Northern went head to head. Additionally, Great Northern's transcontinental main line through Spokane provided seamless connections to the Kootenays from across the USA.

In particular, Great Northern provided Rossland and Trail direct connections to the mining and railway exchanges in San Francisco, Chicago and Spokane. The San Francisco Stock Exchange had been founded in 1862 primarily to trade in mining stocks, and the Chicago Stock Exchange, founded in 1882, handled utilities, banks and railroad companies. The Spokane Stock Exchange, founded in 1892, concentrated on the mining stocks of the Kootenays and the Silver Valley in Idaho. Investors and bankers were the targeted audiences of the railways for business travel.

GN's Red Mountain Railway operated two trains daily between Rossland and Newport, with close connections and through cars to Spokane. The day train departed Rossland at 10:45 am, arriving in Spokane at 5:10 pm. Trail passengers could take the morning Columbia & Western train to Rossland, arriving at 9:15 am. The CP and GN depots were only a block apart, allowing ample time to transfer and catch the 10:45 Spokane departure. Spokane became a favourite destination for the Rossland and Trail locals, offering the best entertainment, dining and shopping in the northwest. Popular weekend excursions offered rail and hotel packages and, in summer, picnic excursions to Northport became the current fashion.[34]

For passengers travelling beyond Spokane, the connections to GN's main line services were excellent. At 8:00 pm, westbound passengers could catch the Puget Sound Express to Seattle, connecting to San Francisco. Eastbound passengers would board

34 Information and schedules from McDonald, *The Railways of Rossland and British Columbia.*

the Eastern Express at 9:25 pm for Minneapolis and Saint Paul, connecting to Chicago.

In the early 1900s, a night train with through car sleepers left Rossland at 11:00 pm, arriving at 6:00 am in Spokane, allowing westbound passengers to connect to GN's crack train, the Oriental Limited to Seattle, a 7:25 am departure. Passengers travelling to Minneapolis, Saint Paul and Chicago would board the eastbound Oriental Limited at 9:15 am. Rossland and Trail, two kingpins in Canada's mining industry, were now easily accessible to the mining magnates and financial gurus of North America.[35]

35   *Information and schedules from the Great Northern Railway Historical Society and Northern Pacific Railway Historical Association Archives.*

TRAINS TO CASTLEGAR

Compared to Nelson, Trail and Rossland, Castlegar got off to a slow start, developing as a town and commerce centre. The surrounding area had few worthwhile mineral deposits. The first settlement in the area, Sproat's Landing, was established in 1888 near the Kootenay and Columbia rivers junction. A dock and warehouse operation received goods transported by CPR sternwheelers from the main line at Revelstoke, serving the new boom town of Nelson and the mines at Toad Mountain. In 1890 construction began on Canadian Pacific's Columbia & Kootenay Railway to Nelson and relocated the transfer point one mile north to a well-drained terrace to provide a better landing. The new terminus was called East Robson, across the river from the current city of Castlegar.

As Grand Forks and Phoenix boomed, rail traffic increased exponentially. The barge service across the river between East and West Robson was the Achilles heel of the system. The solution was a rail bridge across the Columbia to link the rail lines. On the bridge's completion in 1902, the East Robson terminal relocated to the junction where the Columbia & Kootenay Railway met the Columbia & Western, and a new station, called Castlegar, was born.

Castlegar's status as a pivotal junction point for the Columbia & Western was immediate. Castlegar's dedicated departures, plus the connecting services from Nelson, fed the busy branch line to Trail and Rossland. The completion of the Crowsnest line west from Nelson to the new mining hotspots of Grand

Forks, Eholt, Phoenix and Midway had daily passenger departures, in addition to the ore, coal and freight trains. Just minutes west of Castlegar, West Robson was the south terminal for CP's Arrow Lakes steamboat fleet, operating daily to Nakusp and Arrowhead. From Arrowhead, twice daily train service linked the Kootenays with the Canadian Pacific main line at Revelstoke. The Castlegar depot became an increasingly busy stop, and a community slowly emerged. In 1902 the Yale Columbia Lumber Company built a sawmill at Westley, near West Robson. The pulp, paper and timber industries continue to be the financial backbone for Castlegar and the area.

In 1909 a day at the Castlegar station began with a bang. Train 359 arrived from Rossland and Trail at 10:20 am. Minutes later, at 10:25, Train 9 from Nelson, the daily service to Grand Forks and Midway, arrived. It was a tight connection for westbound passengers. Eastbound passengers were hurried, boarding Nelson Train 356 at 10:35 am. Immediately after arrival, Train 359 was turned on the Castlegar wye. It became Train 360, returning to Trail and Rossland, at 10:35 with passengers from Nelson and local workers destined for the smelter and the mines. It was a mad scramble every morning.[36]

There was no further passenger activity during the day, but it was frantic once again in the early evening, with a cluster of arrivals and departures between 7 and 11 pm. At 7:00 pm, the SS *Rossland* or the SS *Minto* from Arrowhead and Nakusp arrived at West Robson, and ongoing passengers would board the awaiting Train 10 from Midway, with arrival in Castlegar at 7:25 pm. Eastbound passengers from Trail and Rossland, who

36   *Schedule information courtesy Steve Boyko, www.traingeek.ca,* CP
System Wide Schedule, 1907.

arrived at Castlegar on Train 355 at 7:05, would board immediately. As soon as Train 10 departed, Train 305 from Nelson
arrived, collecting any northbound passengers from Trail and
Rossland for the five-minute transfer to West Robson to board
the overnight steamer for Nakusp and Arrowhead, which departed at 11:00 pm. Train 355 by this time had been turned and
was now train 360, returning to Trail and Rossland. It was quiet
through the night, followed by another hectic morning.

ARROWHEAD AND NAKUSP:
THE NORTH KOOTENAY GATEWAY

Nelson was the main divisional point for the CPR in southern British Columbia and headquarters for the Kootenay and
Columbia Steamboat fleet. The Arrowhead–Nakusp connection was the pivotal north–south gateway. The flow of
goods, materials and passengers to the mines and railways of
Sandon, Kaslo, Nelson, Trail and Rossland all passed through
this connection.

During the construction of CP's Columbia & Kootenay
Railway in 1891, all equipment, machinery, rails, locomotives,
passenger and freight cars were transported by the Columbia
and Kootenay Steam Navigation Company's sternwheelers
from the main line at Revelstoke, down the Columbia River,
through the Arrow Lakes to Sproat's Landing. At that time,
neither Arrowhead nor Nakusp townsites existed. But in 1891
the CPR built a branch line from Revelstoke to a terminus on
upper Arrow Lake to bypass a treacherous stretch of rapids
on the Columbia. The new rail line eliminated the steamboat
service to Revelstoke, and the new "port" and community
was named Arrowhead. In 1892 the BC government granted
the Nakusp & Slocan Railway charter, and the Nakusp townsite grew. The CPR immediately leased the charter and began
constructing a line into the "Silvery Slocan" to access the developing mines. In 1894 the rail line was completed to Three
Forks and extended to Sandon in 1895. The Arrowhead and
Nakusp townsites continued to grow as mining development

in the Slocan mushroomed. In 1892 the Leland Hotel opened to accommodate arriving travellers and has never closed its doors, considered the oldest continuously operating hotel in British Columbia. The growth of Nakusp fed on the new port development and railway terminus, but soon sawmills and pole yards sprung up along the waterfront, and the logging industry boomed.

The Arrowhead–Nakusp axis was the essential cog in the hub and spoke concept feeding the main line to the north and the Kootenays to the east and south. While Columbia and Kootenay Steam Navigation had been a good partner, reliance on another entity to provide the essential water transportation was regarded as a liability and a potential competitor. That philosophy spurred the CPR to purchase all CKSN assets in 1897, including the Arrow and Kootenay lakes shipyards. That same year, CP built a branch line from Nelson to Slocan City, connecting to the Nakusp & Slocan Railway at Rosebery via steamer, the SS *Slocan*, on Slocan Lake. The new connection solved two operational problems. First, each winter brought freeze-ups on stretches of Arrow Lakes, but Slocan Lake was too deep to freeze, thereby guaranteeing year-round service to Nelson and the South Kootenays. Secondly, it provided a faster and more convenient route to ship ore from Sandon and area mines. Ore cars could now be loaded at Sandon, hauled by rail to Rosebery and then barged to the Slocan City railhead.

One final link remained to dominate the Kootenays, which fell into CP's hands with the demise of the Kaslo & Sandon narrow-gauge railway. Great Northern had tried to sell the damaged line to CP in 1911, but CP had no interest in a narrow-gauge line and no interest in accommodating James J.

Hill. Hill then sold the line at a pittance to a group of Kaslo mine owners, but they lacked the funds to rebuild the line to Sandon. Finally, the BC government became involved, offering a subsidy if the CPR would take over. By 1914 the line had been rebuilt from Parapet to Kaslo in standard gauge. Canadian Pacific finally surrounded the Kootenays, and its fleet of steamboats "ruled the waves."

The July 2, 1914, edition of the *Kootenaian* covered the official opening from Kaslo to Nakusp:

> Regular through freight and passenger service on the Kaslo–Nakusp line will be commenced on Wednesday, July 15 in an announcement by W.O. Miller, Divisional Superintendent. Service will be tri-weekly, the train to connect with the Arrow Lake boats, cutting in half the travel time between here and Vancouver.
>
> Over 300 Kasloites were passengers to Nakusp yesterday, being guests of the Canadian Pacific upon the formal opening of the Kaslo–Nakusp line, set by Geo. Bury, 2nd Vice President, for Dominion Day. The equipment of the train carrying the visitors was the best procurable consisting of five vestibule coaches and one combination baggage and passenger car. In addition, the train had one caboose and the private car of Superintendent Miller, making a total of eight cars in all. As the long train steamed into Nakusp, the shrill whistle from the tugs on the waterfront, the deep bass note of the steamer Bonnington and dynamite salutes ashore greeted the arrival. The hospitable citizens of the flourishing town were everywhere on hand to extend a welcome to the sister community across the Selkirk range. The run was

made in little more than four hours, without mishap and proved a revelation and delight to every passenger.[37]

Daily departures to Nakusp and Arrowhead were now available from all communities in the Kootenays. From the south, an evening sailing at 11:00 pm from West Robson on the ss *Rossland* or *Minto* (and, after 1914, the magnificent ss *Bonnington*) would take passengers from a connecting train from Midway, Phoenix and Grand Forks, and trains from Nelson, Rossland and Trail. The steamer would arrive in Nakusp at 11:50 am the next day, where connections were available by rail to Sandon. The steamer continued to Arrowhead, arriving at 2:50 pm. A one-hour train ride delivered passengers to the main line in Revelstoke. At 5:30 pm, westbound passengers could board the Pacific Express for Vancouver, arriving the following day. In Revelstoke, eastbound passengers overnighted, taking the Eastern Express at 8:30 am for Calgary, Regina, Winnipeg, Toronto and Montreal.

Kootenay-bound passengers arriving in Revelstoke on the Eastern Express would board the 8:50 am departure to Arrowhead. At 10:10, the awaiting steamer departed for Nakusp, arriving at 12:50 pm. In Nakusp, southbound passengers remained on board, arriving at West Robson at 8 pm. The train to Sandon left Nakusp at 1:35 pm. In Rosebery, New Denver, Slocan City and Nelson, passengers boarded the ss *Slocan*. On reaching Slocan City, a connecting train awaited at the dock, departing at 5:55 pm, arriving in Nelson at 7:45 pm. Similarly, Kootenay-bound passengers arriving at Revelstoke

37   *The Kootenaian, July 2, 1914, courtesy Kootenay Museum and Archives, Kaslo, B C.*

from eastern Canada on the Pacific Express would board the same 8:50 am departure for Arrowhead and points south after spending a night in Revelstoke.

The CPR had mastered scheduling and interline connections, providing the public with an incredible transportation network. One hundred years ago, you could travel on scheduled service from any point in the Kootenays to another. While today's highways do access most communities, try doing it without a car. Public transportation today is virtually nonexistent.

THE TRAVELLERS OF YESTERDAY

Today, the distant world of their grandparents (and great-grand-parents) must seem like the Stone Age for many young adults. Then, the closest thing to a computer was a slide rule, the internet did not exist and there were no cell phones. A "text" referred to a book or a written piece of work. Airplanes were just learning how to take off, and there were few long-distance highways, let alone Uber and rental cars. Travellers? Are you kidding? How could they travel to the Kootenays if there were no airports or roads? Very simply, there were lots of options.

Canadian Pacific completed the construction of the trans-continental main line in 1885. The railway initially targeted business travellers and immigrants who would develop and populate the West to increase ridership and revenue for the passenger trains. But Van Horne was a visionary, and he led an infant Canada into the world of tourism. Recognizing the spectacular scenery through the Canadian west as an international drawing card that would augment business travel, he envisioned a chain of first class hotels across the country, all connected by the luxurious passenger trains of the CPR. Van Horne famously stated, "If we can't export the scenery, we'll import the tourists," and by the 1890s had opened the Banff Springs Hotel, the Chateau Lake Louise, Mount Stephen

House in Field, BC, and Glacier House in the middle of the Rogers Pass. Canadian Pacific was the foremost promoter of Canadian tourism and continued to lead the industry through the 20th century.

By 1908 the City of Nelson was lobbying the CPR and the BC government to build the rail line from Kootenay Landing to Procter, providing an all-rail route from Medicine Hat's main line per the Crowsnest agreement. But the Bankers' Panic of 1907 saw US markets crash after the collapse of Knickerbocker Trust, New York's third-largest trust, with a chain reaction spreading to banks across the nation as depositors in the thousands scrambled to withdraw their funds. Two years of slow recovery followed a harsh recession. At that time, Canadian Pacific was unable to entertain the massive expense required to build a rail line along the rugged west shore of Kootenay Lake, preferring to stay with the more economical Crow Boat sternwheelers operating between Kootenay Landing and Procter. Instead, CP offered Nelson a "carrot," offering to build a first class hotel like its famous Rockies resorts in Banff and Lake Louise, spurring tourism in the Kootenays. Nelson Council lobbied hard for the hotel within the city limits. Locals were stunned when Canadian Pacific wielded the "stick," announcing in 1910 the choice of Balfour as the site for the Kootenay Lake Hotel.

In an interview, author and historian Tom Lymbery explains, "CPR's proposal also included building large and luxurious sternwheelers; the *Bonnington* for Arrow Lake, the *Sicamous* for the Okanagan and the slightly larger *Nasookin* for Kootenay Lake. The hotel was constructed on a bluff above Balfour, overlooking the lake and the west arm to Procter, the location chosen to benefit CP's rail and boat transportation system. The new hotel was central to Kootenay Landing, Proctor and Kaslo."

CP's tourism strategies were famously successful, targeting the first class carriage trade to ride its trains to exotic destinations, offering deluxe hotels and amenities on arrival. The hotel would introduce the grandeur of the Kootenays to the world, a strategy Great Northern could not match. For a short first season, the Kootenay Lake Hotel opened to great local fanfare on September 8, 1911.

On September 8, Nelson's *Daily News* reported:

> Construction costs had initially been estimated at $140,000.00 but ballooned to $250,000.00 at completion. An electric cable railway transported passengers from the boat landing to the hotel, which overlooks the west arm across to Procter. Surrounding the building is a pavilion twelve feet wide with hardwood floors. In the basement, two steam-powered generators provide electric power for the hotel and the cable car. Twin boilers provide for heating. Also located in the basement are storerooms and the hotel bakery. The bakery feature is an oven half as large as a common room. The oven temperature is recorded by a thermometer outside, placed conveniently. All bedrooms will be made as homelike as possible, are furnished on a scale of convenience and comfort that cannot but delight the most fastidious. Large beds, excellent fittings, roomy closets, presses and baths, and comfortable furniture will warm the tourist's heart to the Kootenay Lake Hotel. Lighting is a feature that has been a foremost thought in the architect's mind, and large windows in elaborate settings are in every room.

In 1912 the hotel opened for the entire season, early June through October. It was a hugely successful year, and business volumes continued to increase through 1913. The hotel was the first step to drawing tourists to the Kootenays, in a strategy mirroring the Canadian Rockies' development of the Grand Resorts, feeding CP's southern main line passenger trains and the Kootenay and Arrow Lakes sternwheelers. It looked like CP Hotels had another winner.

Unfortunately, timing is everything and early tourism efforts in the Kootenays were dealt a harsh blow on July 28, 1914, when the world went to war. In October the Kootenay Lake Hotel closed its doors, never reopening as a resort. In 1917 the property became a veteran's hospital and tuberculosis sanitarium. "When the lease expired in 1922, the hotel sat empty until 1929. Then it was offered to a contractor for demolition and salvage."[38] It was a sad ending for a gracious resort.

Despite the closure of the Kootenay Lake Hotel, visitors were increasing, coming from all walks of life; some were looking for work, some prospectors and some legitimate tourists. In 1921 a young traveller named Roy E. Green described his journey from Moose Jaw, Saskatchewan, to visit his relatives in Kaslo, BC. Born in Ontario, he worked on the prairies in 1921. On Roy's journey to Kaslo, he travelled by train and steamboat, experiencing easy connections, helpful and courteous staff and affordable hotel accommodation. And it all worked without email, cell phones or texting! By 1921 the larger and more elegant SS *Nasookin* had replaced the SS *Kuskanook* as the Crow Boat connecting the train from Kootenay Landing to Nelson.

Roy Green describes his journey:

38   Art Joyce, "Heritage Beat," *Nelson Daily News*, May 22, 1998.

My return fare from Winnipeg would cost me $20 plus half a cent a mile from where I had worked. That deal expired around the end of October. I had a matter of two or three weeks' leeway before the expiration date. As a youngster, I lived in an environment my mother created for me, the family's story amongst the great Rocky Mountains and Lake Kootenay. Having lived with a scrapbook illustrating this part of the country, I was moved to take advantage of this two weeks' time and pay them a visit. So I dropped the granddad a line and told him I'd be on my way. He wired back and said he'd be delighted to have me come out, so I bought a ticket from Moose Jaw to Kaslo. The trip from Moose Jaw to the foot of the lake was very pleasant. The railroad had just been built through the Crow's Nest Pass [*sic*]. The rolling stock was in pretty fair shape. We had a dining car, and we were pretty well fed. I lived out of a lunch box from Eyebrow until I hit Moose Jaw and the train, so we had a very pleasant trip through the Crow. An exciting time when we came across the prairies and came within sight of the foothills. First time I had ever seen the hills. The foothills just excited me tremendously as a taste of what was to come. I don't think I took my eyes off the scenery from when we came into the foothills and into the Crow's Nest Pass [*sic*] until I hit Kootenay Landing. The transition from the train to the boat was a little exciting. First time I had seen a steamboat the size of the *Nasookin*. She was a three-decker and quite a magnificent ship and comparatively new. Many passengers on the train transferred to the boat. There was a big hustle and bustle on the dockside, at Kootenay Landing, and rattle of the freight carts and the shouting and the puffing of the train and the excitement of the passengers leaving the boat to board the train going east. My fellow passengers left the train, boarding the ship to go west. The excitement of hunting your baggage up and looking after the extra parcels you carried. More especially, you were entering a new phase of life where the scenery, people, and travel were totally different from what you'd been accustomed to. Any rate, we boarded the *Nasookin* about four-thirty in the afternoon, bound for Nelson. And we had time to go aboard, and after the train trip you found it necessary to wash up a little bit, and I had some spare clothes in my suitcase so that I could change my clothes and get rid of the dirty, sooty clothes I'd been wearing on the train. The dinner gong went, and we were assigned our places at the tables. The *Nasookin* was a palatial ship, and the dining room was well laid out. There were sitting accommodations for about 80 diners at a time. The sparkling linen, the vast array of silver, the pose of the stewards in their white jackets and serviettes over their arms. Clean-cut fellows. Looking very professional. The whole deal tended to make me a little bit nervous cause I had mentioned before, we were born on the wrong side of the tracks, we'd been living in poverty the greatest part of my life, and this was a brand new experience for me, so I was a little bit taken aback. One of my great worries was that I might make a little bit of a fool of myself in the presence of company who were evidently well-travelled people and knew their way around. I knew they wouldn't have any difficulty with the silverware especially. But I soon put the nervousness aside because the stewards seemed to be very perceptive to a person's feelings if they were at all nervous. Stewards perceive this quite readily, and so came time to order. I ordered what I thought would be a good starter. I found myself taken care of very well by the steward. If I showed any hesitation, I found myself with the right tool in my hand at the right time. I was unaware that the menu was laid out to have as much or as little as you pleased. But when I found the stewards were pressing me to have not one course, not two courses but all the entrees, the whole deal, I proceeded to take advantage of it. I was 21 years old, and having spent the greater part of my life semi-hungry, this was a great treat. I ate my way halfway from Kuskanook to Nelson for a dollar and a half. When the steward asked me what I'd have for dessert, I looked over the menu and decided deep apple pie would be a new experience to top the whole deal off. I knew enough about apple pie to know that a slice of cheese would go good with it. So I said deep apple pie please, with a slice of cheese. Lo and behold, when they served the apple pie, along came a whole cake of cheese. A round cake of cheese. I suppose it had twenty pounds in it. With a scoop. Now, he says, help yourself. The most liberal helping of cheese I ever had in my life. I didn't go through the whole thing, but I made fair headway with it. Okay. It was in the fall of the year. Dusk came early in that clime, and we had time. We were supposed to dock in Nelson at 9 o'clock in the evening. Dusk set in around about 6 o'clock cause we were in the shelter of the hills. We had plenty of time to communicate. Wander around. Get acquainted with the rest of the passengers. I found them all very fine people. Some of them from every walk of life, and many aristocrats from the old country came into the country to settle or visit. All delightful people. We entered the West Arm, and the West Arm was sparsely settled at that time. Mainly fruit ranchers and some loggers, and others just stump ranchers. There was no highway communication, so the boats took the passengers up from the shore and into town or delivered them to another shore. And it was a most welcome sight on this dark night to see the yellow gleam of very often coal oil lights or candlelights in the cabin windows. I suppose that many of the settlers along the line had an agreement with the boat crews that they would leave their lights burning so they would act as a sort of a beacon so they could plot their course down the river, cause the river was rather treacherous. It formed sandbars that were always shifting, and the boat drew considerable draft. Not excessive draft that you would get on a deep water boat, but 5 or 6 feet, and, of course, this meant that the Masters, the steersman, had to be very careful. Buoys, light buoys laid out the course of the channel, so the captains were very familiar with it, and there was not very much danger of running ashore. But, as I say, the settlers did leave a light burning so it would help the crew.

We arrived in Nelson at 9 o'clock, approximately on time, and it seemed that half of Nelson was down at the dock to meet the passenger train coming in. There were some horse-drawn vehicles, the side-seat type, and others were cab type. They called out the names of the hotels they were soliciting passengers for and I did not have any prior advice as to what was good and bad. I listened to one old-timer with a horse-drawn vehicle. He was calling for the Royal Hotel. Royal sounded pretty good, so I grabbed it and found myself in more or less of a fleabag when we got up that far.

But there was no backing out at that time, and I was shown to a room on the upper floor with a barred window, higher than my head. So I pulled the washstand over against the window to look through the bars to see what the prospect was below in case of fire. I found out that there was nothing for three stories down. Anyway, I couldn't have got through the bars, so I spent a rather uncomfortable night because of wooden hotels, and the old-time hotels had a great record for burning down. At any rate, daylight came, and I had a half day to spend in Nelson until 4:30 in the afternoon when the boat left for Kaslo. I took the *Kuskanook* from Nelson to Kaslo. We left at 4:30 and arrived at Kaslo at 9:30 in the evening. I enjoyed that trip. I had another dinner on board. Very lovely and the people coming into town on that trip. I knew that if I was going into town that I'd be getting acquainted with people at any rate. So being an easterner and a little bit curious, and not having become acquainted with the code of the West, that you "greet people, you're friendly with people, but you don't ask them their business, and you don't ask them where they came from. You simply accept them the way they are." But I was nosy at any rate, and I decided I'd make as many friends as possible on the trip that I could. And I did. I was very successful. Meeting four or five nice people, and when they heard where I was going and who my people were, I received an additional welcome.

We made the usual stops along the lake and arrived opposite Kaslo, at Lighthouse Point, and the town had come into view. I was amazed. I thought I was coming into a village of five or six hundred people, you know. I was amazed. There were lights strung. Streets were lit, and it seemed to be high ground, and it looked like a metropolis, like New York, that we were coming into.

The boat whistled, and we got stirred around to get our baggage in line, and finally, we were arrived in the [Kaslo] Bay at the dock. Half of the town was down there. They were calling out for the King George Hotel. The freight man, the expressman, he was calling out for baggage. People to go up to town. My granddad met me at the dock. Gave me a very, very fine welcome. He arranged with the dray man, a fellow named John Strawn, to pick up my trunk and the rest of my baggage and deliver it to the house. We walked; we didn't ride.[39]

Many Kootenay residents were frequent travellers, using the network of steamboats and trains for business, shopping trips to Nelson, visiting friends and relatives, or for the annual vacation. It was my pleasure to meet Tom Lymbery of Gray Creek, BC, 92 years young, prolific author, regular columnist for the *East Shore Mainstreet* and president of the Gray Creek Historical Society, while researching this book. I had hit the wall trying to source some local data and anecdotes. Fortunately, a mutual friend led me to Tom, who graciously filled in many of the blanks that had me stumped. During one of our meetings, Tom

39   Roy Green, audio transcription, courtesy Kootenay Lake Historical Society, Kaslo, BC.

related the story of an annual family holiday in the Kootenays in the early 1930s.

Tom's father, Arthur Lymbery, was a First World War veteran. While he'd been fortunate to survive four years of horrific warfare, the damp and cold of living in the trenches had done its damage. He suffered from rheumatism in his lower body for the rest of his life. But, happily, Mr. Lymbery found relief in the soothing waters of a Kootenay hot spring. So, after the apple picking season was over in the fall, the Lymbery family journeyed to Halcyon Hot Springs on upper Arrow Lake, north of Nakusp.

During an interview, Tom recalls, "We'd take the steamer from Gray Creek to Proctor in the morning and, after a short visit with friends, caught the afternoon sailing to Kaslo, arriving about 8:00. I'm not sure where we overnighted in Kaslo, but we'd board the train in the morning, arriving in Nakusp just before noon. It was a quick connection to the awaiting steamer, the SS *Minto*, and arrived at Halcyon Hot Springs a couple of hours later. We booked into the hotel at Halcyon and stayed a week. Dad took several dips in the hot baths and pool every day, taking treatments from the in-house medical staff. My sister and I spent a lot of time in the hot pools and exploring the woods around the hotel. The only connection to the outside world was the steamers; there were no roads back then. By the end of the week, we were ready to go home! But Dad loved his visits to Halcyon."

As recounted by the Arrow Lakes Historical Society, "Halcyon gained an international reputation as a place of healing. The bottling works shipped water everywhere. The Workman's Compensation Board sent miners there to sweat out the lead metal. A room became filled with crutches and wheelchairs from people who no longer needed them when they left. Advertised to cure nervous and muscular disorders, liver, kidney and stomach ailments, Halcyon claimed to be the most complete health resort on the continent. Doctors and attendants were on hand at the pools. The Lithia content of the water is unsurpassed by any known spring, and besides being a natural relaxant, was thought to help purify the blood. One man who ran the general store at Halcyon claimed the water caused his hair to grow back."[40]

After a week at Halcyon, Tom looked forward to the trip home. "It was another adventure. We departed from Halcyon mid-morning, sailing to Nakusp and reboarding the train, but we did not return through Kaslo. Instead, we left the train at Rosebery and boarded the SS *Slocan*, steaming the length of Slocan Lake to Slocan City, where we boarded another train to Nelson and spent the night. After Mom had completed her shopping the next day, we took the Greyhound to Balfour, where the bus was loaded onto the SS *Nasookin*, ferrying us across the lake to the Gray Creek Wharf. Our home was below the Gray Creek Store, and the pier was in our backyard. Our holiday was pretty much a tour around the West Kootenays."

When Tom finished high school, he was already a seasoned traveller on the Kettle Valley Railway to Vancouver. The one-room school at Gray Creek only accommodated students through the eighth grade, and in September of 1942, Tom enrolled at North Shore College in Vancouver. The trip to Vancouver was on Greyhound, which he preferred to the train, but as the Second World War progressed, strict rationing curtailed the long-distance Greyhound routes, and Tom then had to travel the train to

40   Rosemary Parent, "The Story of Halcyon Hot Springs," *Arrow Lakes Historical Society*, https://alhs-archives.com/articles/the-story-of-halcyon-hot-springs/.

get home. "We had to use the smoky Kettle Valley steam train at Christmas. They chivvied us into old wooden cars kept at the far end of the train; otherwise, the wooden cars might fold up if they were between more solid cars. Short-distance travellers always got the air-conditioned coach up front with reclining seats, for if they were at the tail end of the train, they would need to unload in the snow. Small stations only had short platforms cleared of snow. If it hadn't snowed for a few days, coal soot covered the snow. There was a cafe car on the train with meals costing a dollar, so I got used to going without eating during the 24-hour trip. (Vancouver had the White Lunch Restaurants with meals costing 15 cents and up)."[41] During our interview, Tom did concede the scenery on the Kettle Valley line was spectacular but at the same time disappointing–the train travelled the Coquihalla portion at night in both directions.

Nicholas Morant's Canadian Pacific, written by J.F. Garden, is possibly the best railway book ever published.[42] Nicholas Morant was internationally famous for his spectacular railway photography and linked forever with the Canadian Pacific Railway. From 1935 through 1981, as the special photographer to the CPR, he was constantly on assignment from coast to coast, photographing the entire CPR portfolio for public relations and advertising purposes. In the 1940s, Nicholas and his wife Willie moved to Banff, and during my working years at the Banff station, I got to know them well. I worked seven summers from 1957 to 1962 as a baggage porter and redcap,

41   Tom Lymbery, *Tom's Gray Creek, Volume 1* (Gray Creek, BC: Gray Creek Publishing, 2013), 169–170.
42   J.F. Garden, *Nicholas Morant's Canadian Pacific* (Revelstoke, BC: Footprint Publishing, 1999).

and we'd regularly load or unload his photographic equipment from the baggage car when he departed or returned from his photo shoots. Willie almost invariably accompanied him, and as Nick said one day during his story time, "Willie is the ablest assistant I've ever had, but also a willing accomplice, so if I go to jail, so will she." We loved his visits as he often regaled us with entertaining stories, laced with a wicked sense of humour, of his experiences across the country.

During such a visit, I asked him, "What is your favourite place in Canada to photograph?" He replied, "Obviously, some of my best work has been in the Rockies [Morant's Curve comes to mind], but I wish I'd been able to spend more time in the Kootenays and along the Kettle Valley route to Vancouver. It is spectacular and the most incredible feat of railway construction in North America. Terry, you must ride that route to Vancouver someday." Sadly, I never did, and now never will. The line through the Coquihalla was closed in 1959 and abandoned in 1961.

SPECIAL TRAINS AND EXCURSIONS

Almost from the day the CPR and Great Northern commenced passenger service in the Kootenays, opportunities awaited to operate special excursion trains. Any travel between the regional communities of Nelson, Kaslo, Trail and Rossland had long been unpleasant ordeals over rough wagon roads, prompted by sheer necessity or emergencies, let alone a trip to Spokane. However, the new freedom of movement sparked by train travel and steamboat networks had caught the public's imagination.

Special trains targeted public holidays, themes and sporting events, including shopping excursions to Spokane or summer picnic outings to favourite locations like Paterson or Northport. Specials became a lucrative source of incremental income. Hockey rivalries were intense between Nelson, Trail and Rossland, and the teams often chartered trains to championship competitions, selling seats to their fans to support them at the games and help offset the price. A $100 deposit secured the booking for a special train, a considerable fee for any team at the time.

After completing the Red Mountain Railway from Rossland to Northport, Great Northern began offering shopping and holiday excursions to Spokane, and they were hugely popular. The variety of stores, goods and services available in the "big city" were unmatched in Kootenay towns and villages. The latest ladies clothing and accessories were available in Spokane, at half the cost of similar products in Canada, if you could even source the goods. The ladies happily patronized organized shopping excursions, and the white collar executives of the mining industry frequented the Spokane haberdasheries. From Rossland, passengers boarded special through cars on the Red Mountain Railway and switched onto GN's Spokane service at Northport. The GN packages included transportation, station transfers and hotel accommodations. The Great Northern agent in Nelson and Kaslo offered similar packages. Steamboat from Kaslo to Five Mile Point connected to GN's Nelson & Fort Sheppard Railway's morning train to Spokane. But among the most popular were the special trains to the Rossland Winter Carnival and Cominco's "Monster" summer picnic at Lakeside Park in Nelson.

ROSSLAND WINTER CARNIVAL AND SPECIAL TRAINS

In 1898 the first Rossland Winter Carnival was a four-day celebration highlighted by winter sports competitions. Ron Shearer, a Rossland historian, has done extensive research into the origins of the carnival. In his essay, "The Rossland Winter Carnival," Shearer credits numerous factors that advanced the idea, including the famous winter carnivals held in Montreal and Quebec City and the inspiration from Rossland's patron saint of skiing, Otto Jeldness, who tirelessly promoted skiing and winter sport. In addition, a large ice rink provided a venue for regional hockey tournaments and skating parties.[43]

As reported on January 18, 1898, in the *Rossland Miner*,[44]

43   Ron Shearer, "The Rossland Winter Carnival," courtesy Rossland Museum & Discovery Centre.
44   Carnival information, Rossland Miner, January and February 1898, courtesy Rossland Museum & Discovery Centre.

"A big winter carnival, such as has not been seen in Canada, is being arranged to take place in Rossland late in February or early in March. All sorts of hibernal sports are included in the program, and a huge snow palace may be constructed, but the great event of the carnival will be the ski running. Skis, as everybody knows, are a Norwegian device, and they have never been equalled for the purpose to which they are adapted. Otto Jeldness is taking much interest in the proposed carnival. Mr. Jeldness, it will be remembered, made a ski run from the summit of Red Mountain to the Le Roi last winter. He is now arranging for some friends, who are excellent ski runners, to be here during the carnival, and together they will make a record-making race from the summit of Red Mountain down into the heart of the town. Moreover, the hockey club is entering into the spirit of the carnival with enthusiasm, and a tourney with the Slocan teams is planned."

The carnival commenced on February 17 through to the 19th. On February 14, 1898, the *Miner* published the schedule of activities:

GRAND WINTER CARNIVAL

- Will Be Held On Friday and Saturday, February 18 and 19, with an opening Carnival Ball held at the Hotel Allan, the evening of February 17.

- Four ski races will be held on Saturday from the summit of Red Mountain, a distance of a mile and a half with a descent of 2000 feet. Open to all!

- To be followed by the Ski Running Championship of Canada on Spokane Street.

- Snowshoe races for the Championship of British Columbia, Skating and Coasting Races.

- Hockey Tournament for the Championship of British Columbia, with a Silver Cup for the winner valued at $100.00 [a small fortune in 1898].

- Grand Curling Bonspiel for Silver Medals.

- Grand Masquerade Carnival in the Palace Skating Rink with prizes for Fancy Costumes will highlight the closing events.

- Special, discounted excursion rates to Rossland from all CPR points in the Kootenays.

- Excursion rates are available from Spokane and all points on the Spokane & Northern Railway and the Nelson & Fort Sheppard Railway.

- All excursion rates valid from February 17 through 21.

The inaugural Rossland Winter Carnival was an unqualified success. The marketing committee, with few resources, did a remarkable job in a short time frame, selling the carnival to sponsors, the railways and the public, both regionally and in Spokane. Whether the "BC or Canadian Championship" monikers for the Rossland events were sanctioned or legitimate was obviously of little importance to the committee. "If you said it first, you owned it," seemed to be the code of the day, and the titles were awarded at the whim of the organizers, attempting to bolster the status of the events. In fact, over time many of the events did become provincial and national championships as the fame of the Rossland Winter Carnival spread across the country.

But the benchmark year was the wildly successful 1899 carnival, held January 27–29. Much of the planning focused on increased visitation from surrounding communities, but Spokane, with a population approaching 40,000, was the number one choice for solicitation. Spokane and Rossland already had close business ties; most corporate and individual investors in the Rossland area mines were Americans, many domiciled in Spokane. In 1899 Rossland was Spokane's most populous and prosperous neighbour, with approximately 7,000 residents, more than twice the population of Coeur d'Alene and the same as Boise, Idaho. Two-way visitation was already well established in the business world. A Rossland delegation successfully presented to the Spokane Chamber of Commerce, which agreed to sponsor a special train during the carnival weekend.

The Saturday, January 28, edition of the *Rossland Miner* reported, "All day yesterday the visitors came pouring in by every means that entered the town, and by evening the hotels were almost practicing the time-honoured expedient of putting their guests to bed on the billiard tables. Great as was the crowd; however, it was but a petty affair besides the attendance today, when not only the Spokane Chamber of Commerce, 200 strong, will arrive on a special train, but the surrounding towns will still further add to their delegations here. It looks as if close to 1,000 strangers will be here to take part in the carnival."

The next day, the *Miner* reported the Saturday arrival of the train from Spokane:

> The Spokane Chamber of Commerce members, with their wives and their sweethearts, came in yesterday afternoon on a special train of four coaches. They had their band with them, and the trip was a lively one. Just

153 visitors started from Spokane, and on the journey, the pilgrims were reinforced with friends picked up at the way stations. The train left Falls City (Spokane) at 8:15 yesterday morning and reached Rossland at 3 pm. At the station, the visitors met a big crowd of revellers headed by Mayor Goodeve and the members of his carnival committee. An impromptu line of march was formed, led by Mayor Goodeve of Rossland and Mayor Olmsted of Spokane. Each of them carried the flag of the other's country. By the way, Rossland probably does more to promote the Anglo-American alliance than any other town in the world. No public celebration is held here unless the Union Jack and the Stars and Stripes are crossed together in a friendly fashion throughout the town. The spontaneous parade continued to the Allan Hotel, accompanied by the band from Spokane, playing hot favourites like, "There'll Be a Hot Time in the Old Town Tonight."

Saturday provided the most exciting events, including the skiing spectacles and the masquerade on ice. But it also marked the surging interest in the hockey tournaments competing for the title of BC Championship, as claimed by the organizing committee. Ron Shearer's essay explains:

Although skiing may have been the main attraction at the first winter carnival, that central position was short-lived. Indeed, as early as 1900, the "Miner" predicted the "the hockey tournament would be the chief feature of the carnival." Hockey became central to the carnival, not just because it appealed to Rosslanders but also because it was the event that attracted trainloads of fans from other cities to support their team. It was also vital to the skating rink. Senior men's hockey packed in the spectators, providing much revenue. Like the carnival itself, the hockey tournament began modestly. However, it soon expanded into women's and junior hockey and began attracting teams outside the Kootenays, including Alberta and across the border in nearby states.[45]

The 1899 Spokane Special departed Rossland on Sunday afternoon. As reported in the *Miner*, "As the visitors wish to reach Spokane tonight in time to catch the late streetcars, the train will leave from here at 3:30 o'clock this afternoon. In the meantime, the guests will have plenty of time to see the most important features of today's program."

Future carnivals included special hockey charters from Trail, Nelson, Cranbrook and even the North-West Territories (Alberta since 1905). Through 1916, the railways continued to offer discounted fares to Rossland in support of the carnival, but through the war years support began to decline, and in 1917 the festival was suspended.

Partly economic, a combination of other occurrences created the perfect storm, leading to the carnival's demise. From a population of 7,000 in 1900, the town was shrinking. There were concerns Rossland might not even survive. In 1917 a devastating coal miners' strike in the Crowsnest forced the Trail smelter to close, shutting down the Rossland mines. The war years seemed to drain public enthusiasm for celebration, and the spectre of the Spanish flu epidemic was raising its head. Raising funds for a carnival in this climate was not going to happen. The famous

45   Shearer, "The Rossland Winter Carnival."

Rossland Winter Carnival quietly disappeared and would not return until 1947. The golden years were over.

ROYALTY VISITS THE KOOTENAYS

Edward, the Prince of Wales and future king, visited Canada in 1919. The visit was official, arranged to thank Canada and Canadians for their enormous sacrifices and contributions to the First World War effort. Prince Edward was immensely popular in Canada, seen as dashing and adventurous, the "new royal" to lead the crown into the 20th century.

During the tour, he became even more beloved as he developed an affinity for all things Canadian, including purchasing a ranch in Alberta before departing back to England. In the 1920s and 1930s, he made private visits to his homestead and did not sell the property until 1962. In a speech in Calgary in 1919, he declared, "I came to Canada as a Canadian in mind and spirit."

Prince Edward sailed from England aboard the HMS *Renown* on August 5, 1919, making landfall at St. John's, capital of the then Dominion of Newfoundland. His arrival at Saint John, New Brunswick, marked a two-month tour across Canada to Vancouver and Victoria, returning to Quebec City.

The Royal Train travelled the CPR main line to Winnipeg, Regina, Calgary, Banff and Vancouver on the westbound journey. Prince Edward travelled CP's Kettle Valley route eastbound, stopping in Penticton with a side trip by sternwheeler to Kelowna, visiting orchards and packing houses. The prince returned to the train for the overnight journey to the Kootenays.

The train arrived in Nelson at 8:30 am on October 1, 1919. After a civic reception, the prince boarded the SS *Nasookin* for Kootenay Landing, with an intermediate stop at Balfour to visit the army hospital and sanitarium, previously CP's

Kootenay Lake Hotel. Here he met with disabled and recovering Canadian troops. Meanwhile, the entire Royal Train, including the locomotive, had been loaded onto railway barges and shipped across Kootenay Lake.

At approximately 8:30 that evening, the *Nasookin* arrived at Kootenay Landing from Balfour. Prince Edward and his entourage boarded the reassembled train and continued the journey east through Cranbrook, Fort Macleod and Lethbridge, rejoining the CP main line at Medicine Hat, Alberta. On November 8, 1919, before reboarding the HMS *Renown* in Quebec to return to England, the prince saluted his "magnificent train":

> I have just left the magnificent train which has transported me across the Dominion and in which I have lived in comfort for the last two and a half months, and I should like to take this opportunity of thanking the Canadian Government for all the admirable arrangements that have been made for the tour. I am also very grateful to all the Canadian Railways for the care they have taken of me and their consideration in making my nine-thousand-mile journey so easy for me. Railways seem to be the subject of quite a lot of excitement at the present moment. I will not talk about that, but I know that I could never get across to Vancouver and back without the Canadian Railways. Far more important still, there would have been no Dominion of Canada today but for them. I know of no country's history where railways have played such an important, in fact, decisively, such a part.

SPECIAL TRAINS TO A SPECIAL PICNIC

During the 1930s, the most anticipated event in Trail and Rossland was Consolidated Mining & Smelting's annual summer picnic. Oddly enough, while the smelter was in Trail and most of the workforce lived in Trail and Rossland, the event was held at Lakeside Park in Nelson. But the location was not shrouded in mystique and was probably chosen by Selwyn Blaylock, the vice-president and general manager of Consolidated Mining & Smelting. Blaylock had a summer home at Robert's Bay, just north of Nelson, and it was by far his preferred residence. The event also became the host city's major event of the year.

The Nelson tradition began in 1931, the idea of Blaylock and Nelson Mayor J.P. Morgan, and continued each summer through 1938. "Joe Hart chaired the original organizing committee, and Mayor Morgan named three other committees to greet the more than 3,000 Trail, Tadanac and Rossland residents expected at the inaugural 'Monster Picnic.'"[46]

The logistics were immense; over 3,000 employees and their families had to be transported to Nelson, returning home in the evening. Canadian Pacific, the parent company, was tasked with scheduling special trains with up to 12 coaches on each departure. In advance of the picnic, CP would requisition extra passenger cars from across the system as far away as Calgary and Winnipeg to meet the commitment. By 1933, 4,100 people attended the picnic, and the numbers peaked in 1937 with over 6,000 attendees.

Of the Monster Picnic, local historian Greg Nesteroff writes,

46   Greg Nesteroff, "CM & S Monster Picnic," The Trail Journal of Local History, Trail Historical Society, 2011.

James J. Hill. COURTESY MINNESOTA HISTORICAL SOCIETY.

Above William Cornelius Van Horne. COURTESY DAVID FLEMING, *ENCYCLOPEDIA OF BANFF HISTORY*, HTTPS://WWW.FACEBOOK.COM/GROUPS/BANFF.HISTORY/.

Facing page, top SS *State of Idaho*, c. 1894. One of the first sternwheelers on the Kootenay River. Photographer unknown. COURTESY TOUCHSTONES MUSEUM OF ART AND HISTORY, NELSON, BC

Facing page, bottom CPR's Columbia & Kootenay Railway, first train to Nelson. COURTESY TOUCHSTONES MUSEUM OF ART AND HISTORY, NELSON, BC.

Corbin's Mountain Station, Nelson, BC.
COURTESY TOUCHSTONES MUSEUM OF ART AND HISTORY, NELSON, BC.

Top Corbin's Nelson & Fort Sheppard train meets Columbia and Kootenay Steam Navigation sternwheeler SS *Nelson* at Five Mile Point, 1893.
COURTESY TOUCHSTONES MUSEUM OF ART AND HISTORY, NELSON, BC.

Bottom Kaslo & Sandon Railway passenger train departs Kaslo station for Sandon.
COURTESY KOOTENAY LAKE HISTORICAL SOCIETY, KASLO, BC.

Top CPR station, Sandon, BC. Foreground behind boxcar, Kaslo & Sandon tracks in background. Pre-1900 fire that destroyed much of the town.
COURTESY TOUCHSTONES MUSEUM OF ART AND HISTORY, NELSON, BC.

Bottom Kootenay Landing train awaits the "Crow Boat" for Nelson, pre-1931.
COURTESY TOUCHSTONES MUSEUM OF ART AND HISTORY, NELSON, BC.

Kaslo & Sandon train crosses trestle near Whitewater, BC.
COURTESY TOUCHSTONES MUSEUM OF ART AND HISTORY, NELSON, BC.

Top SS *International*, Kaslo Bay Wharf, Kaslo & Sandon loading dock.
COURTESY KOOTENAY LAKE HISTORICAL SOCIETY, KASLO, BC.

Bottom Flagship, Kootenay Railway and Navigation Company, SS *Kaslo* nearing completion at Mirror Lake shipyard, 1900.
COURTESY TOUCHSTONES MUSEUM OF ART AND HISTORY, NELSON, BC.

Top SS *Moyie* on an excursion, c. 1908. Dill family album.
COURTESY TOUCHSTONES MUSEUM OF ART AND HISTORY, NELSON, BC.

Bottom SS *Moyie*, Kaslo, BC, 2020. PHOTO T. GAINER.

Top First train from Nelson to Slocan City, 1897. Nelson's first station partly visible, far right. COURTESY TOUCHSTONES MUSEUM OF ART AND HISTORY, NELSON, BC.

Bottom Passengers awaiting Great Northern arrival at Mountain Station. S.M. Bunyan Album. COURTESY TOUCHSTONES MUSEUM OF ART AND HISTORY, NELSON, BC.

Top Canadian Pacific's new depot, Nelson, BC, 1901.
COURTESY TOUCHSTONES MUSEUM OF ART AND HISTORY, NELSON, BC.

Bottom Rail yard and tracks to new wharf, Nelson, BC, c. 1914.
COURTESY TOUCHSTONES MUSEUM OF ART AND HISTORY, NELSON, BC.

CPR station, Nelson, BC, c. 1920.
COURTESY TOUCHSTONES MUSEUM OF ART AND HISTORY, NELSON, BC.

Top CPR and Nelson city wharf.
COURTESY TOUCHSTONES MUSEUM OF ART AND HISTORY, NELSON, BC.

Bottom CPR station, Nelson, BC, 2020. PHOTO T. GAINER.

Above CPR station, Nelson, BC, c. 1920. COURTESY TOUCHSTONES MUSEUM OF ART AND HISTORY, NELSON, BC..

Left Soo-Spokane Train Deluxe, drumhead on rear of observation cars. COURTESY EMORY LUEBKE, SOO LINE HISTORICAL AND TECHNICAL SOCIETY, APPLETON, WI.

"Soo" Line

MINNEAPOLIS
AND
ST PAUL
TO

CHICAGO
BUFFALO
MONTREAL
BOSTON
PORTLAND
NEW YORK
AND THE
EAST

SOLID DAILY TRAIN SERVICE

BAGGAGE checked from a point IN THE UNITED STATES to another point in the States, THROUGH CANADA, does not require inspection.

"Soo" Line

BETWEEN
CHICAGO MILWAUKEE
ST PAUL & MINNEAPOLIS
AND VIA
PORTAL & WINNIPEG
GATEWAYS
TO AND FROM
MANITOBA
WESTERN CANADA
KOOTENAY
SPOKANE
PORTLAND
NORTH PACIFIC COAST

SOLID DAILY TRAIN SERVICE

BAGGAGE checked from a point IN THE UNITED STATES to another point in the States, THROUGH CANADA, does not require inspection.

Facing page, top Soo-Spokane Train Deluxe observation car, 2020.
PHOTO T. GAINER. COURTESY CRANBROOK HISTORY CENTRE.

Facing page, bottom Interior, Soo-Spokane observation car, 2020.
PHOTO T. GAINER. COURTESY CRANBROOK HISTORY CENTRE.

Above Soo Line brochure, Soo-Spokane Train Deluxe.
COURTESY EMORY LUEBKE, SOO LINE HISTORICAL AND TECHNICAL SOCIETY, APPLETON, WI.

Augustus Heinz, entrepreneur, builder of the Trail smelter and first railway to Rossland.
COURTESY TRAIL MUSEUM AND ARCHIVES.

Left Train on the Canyon Creek Trestle, Kettle Valley Railway. COURTESY CRHA/EXPO-RAIL, CANADIAN PACIFIC RAILWAY COMPANY FONDS, MONTREAL.

Below Only the pilings remain at Lardeau, 2021. The rail line to Gerrard followed the left shore. PHOTO T. GAINER.

Remains, CP dock and tracks at Kaslo, 2021. PHOTO T. GAINER.

Top Heinz's Columbia & Western work train building line to Rossland.
COURTESY TRAIL MUSEUM AND ARCHIVES.

Bottom Heinz's Columbia & Western first train to Rossland.
COURTESY TRAIL MUSEUM AND ARCHIVES.

Top Canadian Pacific's daily scheduled Trail – Rossland train, passing through the Gulch. COURTESY TRAIL MUSEUM AND ARCHIVES.

Bottom Great Northern train from Rossland crossing Columbia River at Northport, WA. PHOTO OF POSTER DISPLAY T. GAINER. COURTESY ROSSLAND MUSEUM & DISCOVERY CENTRE.

Top CPR Castlegar bridge nears completion, 1902, linking the Columbia & Kootenay Railway with the Columbia & Western Railway. PHOTO WILLIAM HALE. COURTESY CITY OF VANCOUVER ARCHIVES.

Bottom Castlegar station, c. 1930. COURTESY THE COLUMBIA BASIN INSTITUTE OF REGIONAL HISTORY, CASTLEGAR STATION MUSEUM AND ROSSLAND MUSEUM & DISCOVERY CENTRE.

Top West Robson station, SS *Minto* and train.
COURTESY ARROW LAKES HISTORICAL SOCIETY, NAKUSP, BC.

Bottom Arrowhead, BC, south of Revelstoke on Arrow Lakes. Passengers walking from train to boat, Dominion Day, c. 1912. COURTESY ARROW LAKES HISTORICAL SOCIETY, NAKUSP, BC.

Top First CPR train, Kaslo to Nakusp, leaves Three Forks, 1914.
COURTESY KOOTENAY LAKE HISTORICAL SOCIETY, KASLO, BC.

Bottom First CPR train from Kaslo arrives at Nakusp, 1914.
COURTESY ARROW LAKES HISTORICAL SOCIETY.

SS *Rossland*, SS *Minto*, SS *Kootenay* awaiting passengers at Nakusp station.
COURTESY ARROW LAKES HISTORICAL SOCIETY, NAKUSP, BC.

Top Kootenay Lake Hotel and touring cars, 1913.
COURTESY TOUCHSTONES MUSEUM OF ART AND HISTORY, NELSON, BC.

Bottom Halcyon Hot Springs, Arthur Lymbery's favourite Kootenay destination, c. 1920.
COURTESY KOOTENAY LAKE HISTORICAL SOCIETY, KASLO, BC.

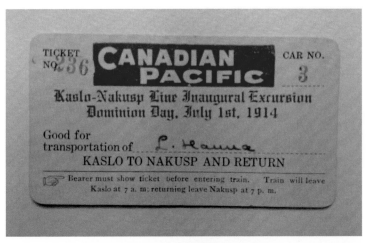

Top Passenger ticket, first train from Kaslo to Nakusp.
PHOTO OF ARCHIVE DISPLAY T. GAINER. COURTESY KOOTENAY LAKE HISTORICAL SOCIETY, KASLO, BC.

Bottom SS *Minto* at CP wharf, Nakusp.
COURTESY ARROW LAKES HISTORICAL SOCIETY, NAKUSP, BC.

Canadian Pacific's Kootenay Lake Hotel at Balfour, BC, c. 1913.
COURTESY TOUCHSTONES MUSEUM OF ART AND HISTORY, NELSON, BC.

Top Nicholas Morant, famous CPR photographer. PHOTO WILLIE MORANT, NICHOLAS Morant Fonds, V2276-1277. COURTESY WHYTE MUSEUM OF THE CANADIAN ROCKIES, BANFF, AB.

Bottom Empire Day special train unloading in Trail, 1914. COURTESY TRAIL MUSEUM AND ARCHIVES.

Top Great Northern train crossing 3rd Avenue trestle, Rossland, BC, c. 1910.
COURTESY THE COLUMBIA BASIN INSTITUTE OF REGIONAL HISTORY, CASTLEGAR STATION MUSEUM,
AND ROSSLAND MUSEUM & DISCOVERY CENTRE.

Bottom Trail hockey team boards special train. COURTESY TRAIL MUSEUM AND ARCHIVES.

The Prince of Wales arrives at Balfour for sanitarium visit with First World War veterans.
COURTESY TOUCHSTONES MUSEUM OF ART AND HISTORY, NELSON, BC.

Top Engineers, firemen and CPR dignitaries posing with Royal Train locomotives.
COURTESY BBC ARCHIVES.

Bottom Consolidated Mining & Smelting employees' picnic, Lakeside Park, Nelson, BC,
1933. COURTESY TOUCHSTONES MUSEUM OF ART AND HISTORY, NELSON, BC.

Top Main gate, train unloading site for Consolidated Mining & Smelting employees' picnic. Note railway tracks in foreground.
COURTESY TOUCHSTONES MUSEUM OF ART AND HISTORY, NELSON, BC.

Bottom Consolidated Mining & Smelting, 1933 picnic.
COURTESY TOUCHSTONES MUSEUM OF ART AND HISTORY, NELSON, BC.

Top Japanese internment train, Slocan City, 1942.
PHOTO CP WIRESERVICE, *THE KOOTENAIAN*. COURTESY KOOTENAY LAKE HISTORICAL SOCIETY, KASLO, BC.

Bottom Internment camp in winter at New Denver.
COURTESY KOOTENAY LAKE HISTORICAL SOCIETY, KASLO, BC.

Top New Denver internment camp.
COURTESY KOOTENAY LAKE HISTORICAL SOCIETY, KASLO, BC.

Bottom Kootenay Express and passengers, Crowsnest station, Crowsnest Pass, c. 1924.
COURTESY CRHA/EXPORAIL, CANADIAN PACIFIC RAILWAY COMPANY FONDS, MONTREAL.

Top The "Galloping Goose" at Mountain Station, Nelson, in winter.
COURTESY TOUCHSTONES MUSEUM OF ART AND HISTORY, NELSON, BC.

Bottom Eric "Pat" Paterson, Kaslo Greyhound driver, ready for the Nelson schedule, 1928.
COURTESY KOOTENAY LAKE HISTORICAL SOCIETY, KASLO, BC.

Top Official Nelson – Kalso highway opening day ceremony, July 28, 1926, Ainsworth, BC. Premier John Oliver and Lieutenant-Governor Randolph Bruce.
COURTESY KOOTENAY LAKE HISTORICAL SOCIETY, KASLO, BC.

Bottom Canadian Pacific rail car and trailers, Lardeau to Gerrard.
COURTESY TOUCHSTONES MUSEUM OF ART AND HISTORY, NELSON, BC.

Greyhound bus on bow of SS *Nasookin* after conversion to Kootenay Lake ferry.
COURTESY KOOTENAY LAKE HISTORICAL SOCIETY, KASLO, BC.

The Kootenay Express steams into Nelson.
COURTESY CRHA/EXPORAIL, ADDISON LAKE FONDS, MONTREAL.

SS *Minto* at Arrowhead unloading passengers for train, passenger posing.
COURTESY ARROW LAKES HISTORICAL SOCIETY, NASKUSP, BC.

Top SS *Bonnington*, pride of Arrow Lakes, luxurious dining room, c. 1920s.
COURTESY TOUCHSTONES MUSEUM OF ART AND HISTORY, NELSON, BC.

Bottom Trout Lake City, c. 1910. COURTESY ARROW LAKES HISTORICAL SOCIETY, NAKUSP, BC.

Top The SS *Victoria*, Gerrard to Trout Lake City steamer.
COURTESY ARROW LAKES HISTORICAL SOCIETY, NAKUSP, BC.

Bottom Nelson's diesel service plant, opened January 29, 1954. *Nelson Daily News*.
COURTESY TOUCHSTONES MUSEUM OF ART AND HISTORY, NELSON, BC.

Top Abandoned CP rail line (Nakusp and Slocan Railway) and bridge, near Rosebery, BC, 2021. PHOTO T. GAINER.

Bottom Abandoned Nakusp and Slocan track bed near New Denver, 2021. PHOTO T. GAINER.

Top SS *Kootenay* and SS *Bonnington* at Arrowhead dock, loading from train, c. 1920s. COURTESY ARROW LAKES HISTORICAL SOCIETY, NAKUSP, BC.

Bottom SS *Slocan* at New Denver wharf.
PHOTO OF MEMORIAL PLAQUE, NEW DENVER, 2021, T. GAINER.

Top SS *Nasookin* passes SS *Moyie* in West Arm, Kootenay Lake, c. 1920s.
COURTESY TOUCHSTONES MUSEUM OF ART AND HISTORY, NELSON, BC.

Bottom SS *Moyie*, Kootenay Lake Hotel, guest in rowboat in foreground.
COURTESY TOUCHSTONES MUSEUM OF ART AND HISTORY, NELSON, BC.

Bridge to Kootenay Landing, c. 1910.
COURTESY TOUCHSTONES MUSEUM OF ART AND HISTORY, NELSON, BC.

Kootenay Landing, train meets the "Crow Boat."
COURTESY TOUCHSTONES MUSEUM OF ART AND HISTORY, NELSON, BC.

Top Postcard, Kootenay Landing, c. 1910.
COURTESY TOUCHSTONES MUSEUM OF ART AND HISTORY, NELSON, BC.

Bottom Kaslo & Sandon train at Whitewater. Note bags of ore on platform.
COURTESY KOOTENAY LAKE HISTORICAL SOCIETY, KASLO, BC.

KOOTENAY RAILWAY & NAVIGATION CO., Ltd.

KASLO & SLOCAN RAILWAY COMPANY.
INTERNATIONAL NAVIGATION & TRADING CO., Ltd.

TIME TABLE NO. 11.

Effective 12:01 a. m. Monday June 11th, 1906.

KASLO & SLOCAN RAILWAY CO.

Second Class NO. 2 MIXED Daily		Miles From Kaslo	STATIONS.	Second Class No 1 MIXED Daily	
Eastbound				Westbound	
Leave 1:30	P.M.	28.2	.... SANDON	Arrive 10:25	A.M.
		27.7	................WOOD	f	.....
f		26.5	........CODY JUNCT........	f	.....
s	1:37	26.3	........PAYNE TRAM........	s	10:15
f		24.8	..........BAILY'S...........	f	.....
s	1:52	22.7	........McGUIGAN...........	s	10:00
f		21.0	.........LUCKY JIM..........	f	.....
f		19.9	...... BEAR LAKE.........	f	.....
s	2:12	18.0	...... WHITEWATER	s	9:25
f	2:25	15.4	.......SPROULES........	f	.....
f	3:15	5.7	...... SOUTH FORK	f	8.30
Arrive 3:45	P.M.		..........KASLO........	Leave 8:00	A.M.

INTERNATIONAL NAVIGATION & TRADING CO.
STEAMER KASLO OR INTERNATIONAL.

Daily Except Sunday		Miles From Kaslo	PORTS	Daily Except Sunday	
Southbound				Northbound	
Leave 5:30	A.M.		..........KASLO.	Arrive 9 25	P.M.
„ 6:30		13.0	...... AINSWORTH....	„ 8:15	
		20.0	...... PILOT BAY.....		
„ 9:20		40.0	...,,TROUP JUNCTION........	„ 6:20	
Arrive 9.40	A. M.	45.0	...........NELSON	Leave 5:45	P.M.

Eastbound trains have absolute right of track over trains of the same or inferior class running in the opposite direction.

General Rules regulating the movement of trains, are contained in Book of Rules for the government of the operating department, a copy of which must be in the hands of each employee in train service while on duty.

Steamers will call at way landings on signal.

This time table is for the information and government of employees only and is not intended as an advertisement of the time or hours of any train or steamer and the Company reserves the right to vary from it at pleasure.

P. H. WALSH,
SUPERINTENDENT.

Kootenay Railway and Navigation Timetable, c. 1898.

PHOTO OF HANDBILL T. GAINER. COURTESY KOOTENAY LAKE HISTORICAL SOCIETY, KASLO, BC.

Top Bus and trucks unload Japanese Canadian prisoners at New Denver camp.
COURTESY KOOTENAY LAKE HISTORICAL SOCIETY, KASLO, BC.

Bottom SS *Kaslo* loads for holiday excursion, Kaslo dock, 1898.
COURTESY KOOTENAY LAKE HISTORICAL SOCIETY, KASLO, BC.

Top SS *Nasookin*, maiden voyage to Kaslo, May 24, 1913.
COURTESY MICHAEL CONE COLLECTION AND KOOTENAY LAKE HISTORICAL SOCIETY, KASLO, BC.

Bottom Train at Canadian Pacific depot, downtown Trail, Cedar Avenue and Farwell Street, 1940. COURTESY TRAIL MUSEUM AND ARCHIVES.

August 13, 1945

Trail Helped in Atomic Bomb - Heavy Water Made in C.M.&S. Plants

The Trail plants of the C.M.&S. Co. of Canada, Ltd., played a part in the production of the atomic bomb it was revealed today by Munitions Minister Howe at a press interview in Ottawa. The Trail plants produced heavy water which is used to control the release of energy in the bomb.

Further details of Trail's part in this gigantic discovery are shrouded in secrecy. So far, censors have refused to divulge anything more about the Trail operation. The Trail Daily Times has appealed to the dominion press censor for some release of information concerning this story but the censor replied that only the minister's words could be used.

C.M.& S. officials, contacted today, said that they were forbidden to discuss the matter.

OTTAWA, Aug. 13 (CP) - The United States is the only country which knows all the details of the atomic bomb, but the information would be made available to Canada and Britain if they should ask for it, Munitions Minister Howe said today.

While Canada made essential parts of the bomb, the Canadian government, for reasons of security, decided not to ask for complete details of the bomb, and the United Kingdom followed a similar course, said Mr. Howe at a press conference in his second floor office of one of Ottawa's temporary buildings.

At the conference with Mr. Howe were Dr. C. J. Mackenzie president of the national research council, Dr. J. D. Cockcroft, formerly of Cambridge university in England and now director of the national research council laboratory in Montreal. Dr. G. C. Laurence of the

national research council in Ottawa, and Dr. N. Kemmer, formerly of London and Cambridge universities and now attached to the research council's Montreal laboratory.

Many Worked in Project

These men were among the many scientists who worked on the development of atomic energy in Canada.

"We haven't asked for details of the bomb," said Mr. Howe. "If we had needed them we would have asked for them and we would have got them. It is a good thing not to have too much information at times."

All information about the possible industrial and peace time uses of atomic energy were being exchanged between the United States, Canada and Britain.

Dr. Mackenzie said the secret of the bomb was one of the best kept of the war. Only a few men knew all the details . . . Canada's part was concerned with the manufacture of essential parts of the bomb. Uranium concentrates from the Great Bear lake area were brought to Port Hope, Ont. and processed there. The processed material went to the research laboratories. No peace time application of atomic energy had yet been attempted, but research was going forward. As an example of atomic energy, Mr. Howe gave this illustration: If one was able to split the coal atom instead of burning coal he would get 1,000,000 more times heat than from coal. Canada will continue her research after the war and the plant at chalk River, Ont. will be a permanent institution. "Atomic energy will be used for the best interests of humanity as a whole," said Mr. Howe . . .

Veiled in secrecy, the best kept secret during the Second World War was the making of heavy water for the atomic bomb, right here in Trail. The Manhattan Project employed workers at Consolidated Mining & Smelting Co. of Canada for the important task, but only a very few people in upper management really knew what was going on. The official report on Trail's involvement wasn't actually fully revealed until 1954. The above photo shows how construction of the building was hidden from view. At the end of the century, the building still stands, unused.   Cominco photo

Trail and the atomic bomb. Consolidated Mining & Smelting heavy water plant. *Trail Daily Times*, December 12, 2000. COURTESY TRAIL MUSEUM AND ARCHIVES.

Above Au revoir Kootenay rails! Bridge and abutment remains, Kaslo & Sandon Railway, near Whitewater, 2021. PHOTO T. GAINER.

Left Canadian Pacific's train and boat service, Kootenay Lake, c. 1906. PHOTO OF CP POSTER T. GAINER. COURTESY TOUCHSTONES MUSEUM OF ART AND HISTORY, NELSON, BC.

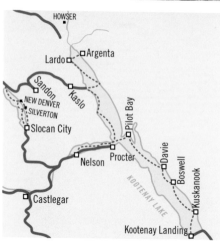

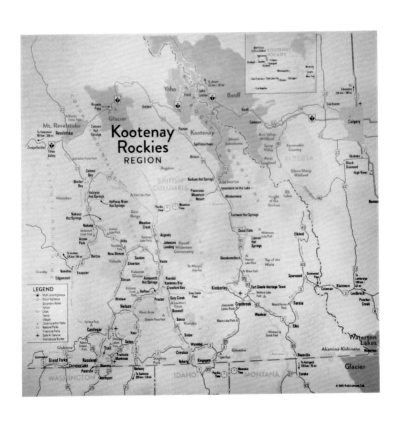

The Kootenays of British Columbia.
COURTESY KOOTENAY ROCKIES TOURISM, KIMBERLEY, BC.

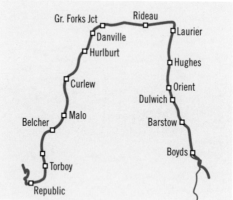

Top Great Northern, Oroville to Princeton. Illustrator James C. Mattson. COURTESY BOB KELLY, GREAT NORTHERN RAILWAY HISTORICAL SOCIETY ARCHIVES, SEATTLE, WA.

Bottom Great Northern, Kettle Falls to Grand Forks to Republic, WA. Illustrator James C. Mattson. COURTESY BOB KELLY, GREAT NORTHERN RAILWAY HISTORICAL SOCIETY ARCHIVES, SEATTLE, WA.

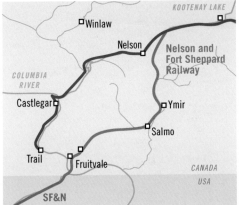

Top Great Northern, Grand Forks to Phoenix spur line. Illustrator James C. Mattson. COURTESY BOB KELLY, GREAT NORTHERN RAILWAY HISTORICAL SOCIETY ARCHIVES, SEATTLE, WA.

Bottom Corbin's railways, Nelson & Fort Sheppard joins his Spokane Falls & Northern at the border. Illustrator James C. Mattson. COURTESY BOB KELLY, GREAT NORTHERN RAILWAY HISTORICAL SOCIETY, SEATTLE, WA.

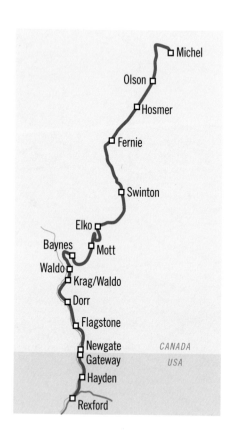

Montana and Great Northern Railway from Rexford, MT, and Crowsnest Southern Railway to Fernie and Michel, BC. Illustrator James C. Mattson. COURTESY BOB KELLY, GREAT NORTHERN RAILWAY HISTORICAL SOCIETY ARCHIVES, SEATTLE, WA.

"A decoration committee ensured every business street of Nelson had a gala appearance for the big event and also that the merchants and citizens cooperated in the decorating. They also looked after erecting temporary shelters at the park, sanitary arrangements, operating the bathing houses, fencing off the beach for children, putting a safety boom in shallow water and providing garbage cans. A reception committee met with the picnic organizers, who came a day early to prepare tables, install ranges for heating water and erect tents. On the day of the picnic, the *Trail Daily Times* reported, 'Under fine weather, residents packed their picnic baskets and invaded Nelson by train, in the biggest known picnic the interior of British Columbia has known.'"[47]

The undertaking was massive and probably would not be possible in today's world of diminishing community spirit and liability concerns that stifle community events. But that was not the world of the 1930s. The Consolidated officials declared a workers' holiday for the picnic date, and only a volunteer skeleton crew remained behind to ensure safety at the Trail smelter.

The 1933 picnic program provided the details of the day's events and train schedule:

Consolidated Mining & Smelting Company of
Canada, Limited
Employee's Third Annual
BASKET PICNIC
LAKESIDE PARK, NELSON, BC
Saturday, July 22nd, 1933

INSTRUCTIONS TO PICNICKERS

47   Nesteroff, "The CM & S Monster Picnic."

General Instructions

- Don't forget your free Transportation Ticket or identity card. You will require it on the train.
- Don't take milk, dry tea, coffee or sugar. Hot water is free for everyone at Lakeside Park. Milk will be provided for babies.
- Take your dishes, cutlery and teapot or coffee container.
- Sports will commence at Lakeside Park at 11:00 am.
- Free streetcar and automobile transportation will be provided between Lakeside Park and the business section of Nelson.
- Refreshments for children are available at Lakeside Park.
- First Aid Tent, Lost Children's Tent, Mother's Rest Room, also Cloak Room will be erected at Lakeside Park.
- Kindly do your best to keep the park clean and refrain from doing any wilful damage.
- Please do not use tables as Wardrobes or Luggage Platforms. They are dining tables ONLY.
- Lost refreshment strip tickets will not be replaced.
- No. 1 Train leaving Trail depot at 7:20 am is reserved for mothers and small children from Trail to Tadanac.
- Each refreshment strip ticket entitles you to the following: ice cream cone, candy, peanuts, pop or milk.
- All passengers must leave the train by the one exit, which will be at Lakeside Park Main Gate. By all means, keep off the railroad tracks.

- Please observe street traffic rules in the City of Nelson to minimize the possibility of accidents.
- The committee hopes you will enjoy yourselves and will appreciate your cooperation.

TRAIN SCHEDULE AND INFORMATION

Trail and Rossland to Nelson
- Train No. 1.
- Trail, 3 coaches; Lv. 7:05 am. Lv. Tadanac 12 coaches.
- Train No. 2.
- 7:00 am. Lv. Rossland City Depot, 4 coaches; 7:05 Lv. Rossland Union Ave. Depot 4 coaches; 8:05 am. Lv. Tadanac, 12 coaches.
- Train No. 3.
- 7:40 am. Lv. Rossland City Depot, 4 coaches; 7:45 Lv. Rossland Union Ave. Depot, 4 coaches.
- Train No. 4.
- 1:40 pm. Lv. Trail, 3 coaches; 2:00 pm, Lv. Tadanac 12 coaches.

Leaving Nelson
- Train No. 1.
- 6:00 pm. Lv. Lakeside Park, Nelson.
- 6:05 pm. Lv. Nelson Depot. 12 coaches, 3 coaches will go to Rossland, 3 will unload at Trail Depot, the balance at Tadanac.
- Train No. 2.
- 7:15 pm. Lv. Lakeside Park, Nelson.
- 7:25 pm. Lv. Nelson Depot. 12 coaches. This train unloads at Tadanac only.
- Train No. 3.

- 7:45 pm. Lv. Lakeside Park.
- 7:50 pm. Lv. Nelson Depot. 12 coaches, 3 coaches will go to Rossland.
- Train No. 4.
- 11:00 pm. Lv. Nelson Depot only. 3 coaches will go direct to Rossland, and all others will unload at Tadanac.

The late train was for the fun lovers and revellers. While there was an evening banquet for organizers and dignitaries who would ride the train back to Trail, the bulk of the evening crowd stayed in Nelson to dine and dance the night away at various Nelson hotels and saloons. As remembered by Glenna Ehman and Val Huth of Trail, "The coaches were always packed with people young and old, and the return trip at night was a happy one ending with laughter and sing-songs."[48]

In 1939 the world was sitting on a powder keg awaiting the inevitable world war, which broke out on September 1. As a result, the annual picnic never returned.

48   Nesteroff, "The CM & S Monster Picnic."

NOT-SO-SPECIAL TRAINS:
CANADA'S SHAME, JAPANESE CANADIAN INTERNMENT

Immigration from Japan to Canada began in 1877. Most immigrants were young men, called Issei, meaning the first generation. In 1908 Canada limited the Japanese migration of males to 400 per year, which meant that most new immigrants were women joining their husbands, or unmarried women engaged to men currently living in Canada. The Issei were primarily young and literate from farm and fishing villages on the southern islands of Kyushu and Honshu. By 1940 Canada's Japanese Canadian population had surpassed 21,000 residents, most born in Canada. The great majority resided in British Columbia in so-called Japantowns in Vancouver and Victoria, fishing villages like Steveston, on farms in the Fraser Valley or pulp and paper company towns along the BC coast. The Japanese Canadians were far from integrated, but, generally, life was good. But on December 7, 1941, Japan bombed Pearl Harbor and attacked Hong Kong, overrunning the Canadian troops stationed there. The events were shocking and fears of a Japanese invasion swept the country. The world changed overnight for Japanese Canadians.

The *Canadian Encyclopedia* describes the mood leading up to the internment:

> The flames, fanned by a sensationalist press spreading stories of distrust, had the public in an uproar. But, of course, there were moderate supporters, including

Major-General Kenneth Stuart: "From the army point of view, I cannot see that Japanese Canadians constitute the slightest menace to national security." However, BC politicians were in a rage and spoke of the Japanese "in the way the Nazis would have spoken about Jewish Germans," said Canadian diplomat Escott Reid. "When they spoke, I felt the physical threat of evil."

In February 1942, the federal Cabinet of Prime Minister William Lyon Mackenzie King issued an order-in-council to remove and detain "any and all persons" from any "protective area" in the country. Those powers were broad enough to apply to anyone. But they were specifically used to target Japanese Canadians along the west coast. The following week, the British Columbia Security Commission was established. It implemented and carried out Japanese internment.[49]

The British Columbia Security Commission selected the Kootenays and neighbouring communities of Grand Forks and Greenwood in Boundary County for relocation villages. Over 21,000 Japanese Canadians were detained, initially in a tent city in Vancouver's Hastings Park. Those who resisted internment spent the war in POW camps in Petawawa, Ontario, or Camp 101, on Lake Superior. The government seized 1,200 fishing boats, and all Japanese Canadians lost their farms, businesses, homes and personal property. The government sold off everything to pay for their internment. Imagine paying for your prison sentence for the crime of having the wrong skin colour.

49   See Greg Robinson, "Internment of Japanese Canadians," The Canadian Encyclopedia, https://www.thecanadianencyclopedia.ca/en/article/internment-of-japanese-canadians.

"I was a 22 year old Japanese Canadian," said Tom Tamagi, "a prisoner of my own country of birth. We were confined inside the high wire fence of Hastings Park just like caged animals."[50]

I met Kaien Shimizu in the early 1960s in Banff. Kaien was a close friend of my brother Fred, and they had met at the University of Alberta and were brothers in the same fraternity. In May 2021, I visited the Nikkei Internment Memorial Centre. While browsing, I came across an article written by Dr. Henry Shimizu, an internee at the camp. The name triggered a faint memory, and I wondered if Henry was related to Kaien. Thanks to my brother and his wife, Connie, I contacted Kaien. I found out Henry was his brother. I've since had the good fortune to interview both of them and learn about the Shimizu family experience. The family spent four years in the New Denver camp. Their story encapsulates the internment of thousands of Japanese Canadians during the Second World War, remembered as one of Canada's darkest hours.

Henry Shimizu was born in Prince Rupert, BC, in 1928, followed by Kaien and two sisters, to Tom and Kimiko Shimizu. Mr. Shimizu and his close friend George Nishikaze owned the Dominion Café and a 30-room hotel. In our interview, Henry stated, "We were not a tight Japanese community in Prince Rupert, unlike Powell Street in Vancouver. The Japanese people were scattered all over. My friends were a multicultural group, Yugoslavian, English, Chinese, Japanese, and Indian girls. My parents worked hard, but we had a good life. But in 1941, before the Pacific War broke out, the Canadian government required us to register. We had to carry ID cards, complete with a thumbprint. Mine was blue because I was 13 years of age and

50   Robinson, "Internment of Japanese Canadians."

Canadian-born. In February of 1942, the situation became tense as the government began issuing the orders-in-council. My father knew something was wrong, so he tried to sell the hotel and restaurant. There were no takers. Then came the first bad news. Ordered to leave Prince Rupert, Dad had to rent the business."

Hastings Park in Vancouver became the destination for all Japanese Canadians removed from locations along the coast, from Prince Rupert to the US border. Those who lived in Vancouver and the surrounding area remained in their homes until removed directly to internment camps. Henry described the Shimizu family's journey:

> Mom and we four children left Prince Rupert by train on March 23, 1942. Papa and Mr. Nishikaze departed a few days before us for a work camp, as did all Japanese males over 18 years of age. At Prince George, we transferred to a different train. It took two days to get to Vancouver, taking a siding directly into Hastings Park.
>
> Simply put, the park, surrounded by a 10-foot, link-wire fence, was a concentration camp. On arrival, the authorities separated our family. The experience became very different. Because I was thirteen, I had to stay in the Forum with the men. My mother, brother and two sisters had to stay in the livestock building. The stalls became makeshift bedrooms and required cleaning because they were full of poop. The smell never went away. Meals, prepared by Japanese staff, were served in a mess hall. Hastings Park was our home for six months. My father kept telling my mother not to move out of BC, that this was all a mistake. Convinced the authorities would

come to their senses, he believed we'd be sent back to Prince Rupert.

After six months, it was evident this was not going to happen. The government had started building in the BC interior. Ten internment camps sprung up around the Slocan Valley in Rosebery, New Denver, Nelson Ranch, Harris Ranch, Sandon, Slocan City, Bay Farm, Popoff and Lemon Creek, the largest camp. Kaslo, on Kootenay Lake, became the administrative centre. Twelve thousand Japanese Canadians lived in the camps. Over 10,000 more Japanese Canadians trained to southern Alberta, Manitoba, Ontario and Quebec, assigned as farm labourers.

We boarded a train for a two-day transfer to Slocan City in September. On arrival, we loaded ourselves and our luggage onto waiting trucks for the rough and terrifying 20-mile journey to some mysterious place called New Denver. We arrived in New Denver before noon. The bags were placed in the middle of a field while we had lunch in a converted curling rink. The front end was the mess hall, and the back end became the carpenter shop. After lunch, we sorted our luggage and were assigned two families to a tent. We shared our tent with the Nishikazes, our family friends from Prince Rupert. Reassigned to New Denver from the men's work camp, my father and Mr. Nishikaze rejoined their families. We were interned but happily together again.

Had it been a different situation, there might have been some humour in their assignment. Dad and Mr. Nishikaze, sent to New Denver to be carpenters, barely knew how to hold a hammer. Their job, building the shiplap houses for the internees, must have proceded by trial and error.

Finally, in November, the housing was ready, and families moved out of the tents. Two hundred and twenty-five shiplap shacks, built in the middle of an orchard, became the camp homes. Our residence, a so-called mid-sized house, had two tiny bedrooms flanked by a slightly larger room. Six Shimizus and five Nishikazes occupied that little shack for the next four years. We had no running water, and the "privy" was out the back. The first winter was brutal; even Mother Nature conspired against us. The 1942–1943 winter was frigid with heavy snowfall. The shacks, constructed of green lumber, dried and shrunk, and the wind seemed to whistle through the cracks. We spent many evenings huddled around the stove, just trying to keep warm. Good food supply was a problem, and local stores were expensive. Fortunately, the Doukhobors were friendly and sympathetic. They were no strangers to persecution and provided us with healthy and inexpensive produce. In the spring of 1943, vegetable gardens were a priority, a task for the women and children. Many apple trees remained, and we became almost self-sufficient. Meanwhile, Dad and the "carpenters" tar papered the shacks and covered the exterior walls with cedar shingles, split by the men from large cedar blocks. That stopped the leaks, adding some semblance of insulation.

Our first summer in New Denver brought some pleasant experiences. It was the first time we had Japanese neighbours, and kids were everywhere. We played baseball and competed with other camps. But the highlight of every summer was the abundance of fresh fruit. The fruit trees were everywhere. We'd never experienced this luxury.

Kaien Shimizu's recollections of the internment included some happy memories: "New Denver was all fun and games for me. We had the lake, lots of kids to play with and the orchards for fresh fruit, and I was very young when the relocation occurred, so I did not feel any of the suffering and worries of my parents. It was the first time in my life to be surrounded by hundreds of other kids, and I was only in grade 2 when we left. When we were in New Denver, I remember the best cherries came from Kaslo."

My interview with Henry Shimizu ended with the harsher realities of Japanese internment.

By 1943 word reached the camps, our properties were sold off, including homes, 1,200 fishing boats and our farms throughout the province. Someone bought our hotel and restaurant, but we never knew who. Even our furniture and possessions were sold or disappeared. The reason given was to pay for the cost of our internment. My parents used the terminology *shikata ga nai* to explain the situation: "It can't be helped." Japanese Canadians simply made the best of their predicament.

At the end of the war in 1945, there was no change to the restrictions on Japanese Canadians. In the USA, interned Japanese Americans were released and returned to their properties owned before the war. The US government safeguarded the properties throughout the war. Not so in Canada. Our camps remained. A powerful coalition of BC politicians determined to move all Japanese Canadians out of BC, allied with business groups to enforce their will. "They" decided Japanese Canadians did not belong in British Columbia.

The Shimizu family relocated to Edmonton when the New Denver camp closed. Henry became one of the first Japanese Canadian doctors in 1954 and then a professor of medicine at the University of Alberta. Dr. Shimizu chaired the Japanese Canadian Redress Foundation from 1989 to 2001. He won many awards for his humanitarian work, including the Order of Canada in 2004.

Kaien Shimizu first graduated in engineering from the University of Alberta. Then he returned to the west coast, graduating from the University of British Columbia in architecture. Kaien had a distinguished career as an architectural consultant and retired to Vancouver Island. In an interesting side note, Kaien revealed his given name is not Japanese. He was born in Prince Rupert, located on the island of Kaien, and his parents chose it to signify his Canadian heritage.

In 1944, after intense questioning in Parliament, Prime Minister Mackenzie King admitted that not one Japanese national or Japanese Canadian was charged with sedition or treason. But even after the war, Mackenzie King continued to bow to the most strident demands of the politicians and citizens he represented. He offered Japanese Canadians two choices: move to Japan, or disperse to provinces east of the Rocky Mountains. He never expressed any regrets for the treatment of Japanese Canadians during the war or after.[51] Internment lasted through the Second World War, but the stigma and suffering continued

51   Robinson, "Internment of Japanese Canadians."

until 1949. That year, after intense pressure on Parliament, Japanese Canadians finally received full citizenship, the right to vote and freedom of movement.

The "not-so-special trains" are part of a horrendous chapter in Canadian history. Japanese Canadian citizens, stripped of their dignity, rights and property, waited over 40 years for the Canadian government to address the issue. Finally, in 1988, Prime Minister Brian Mulroney apologized for its wrongs against Japanese Canadians on behalf of the government. The government also made symbolic redress payments and repealed the War Measures Act. But a thousand apologies could never make up for the loss of property, businesses, humiliation and mistreatment 21,000 Canadians had to endure in their own country.

In hindsight, internment highlights the insanity of war. The Japanese Canadian Internment was a nightmare Catch-22 situation. Imprisoned for no crime but unable to go to prison until you build it. Then you have your illegally confiscated possessions sold to pay for the construction and maintenance of your self-built penal colonies. We must never forget the lessons of history.

INTO THE 20TH CENTURY

By 1911 a sense of change was in the air. Great Northern had quietly conceded to Canadian Pacific in the Battle for the Kootenays, liquidating the Kootenay Railway and Navigation Company and selling the Kaslo & Sandon Railway. By 1913 the Bedlington & Nelson Railway from Kuskanook to the border near Creston removed its tracks, ceasing operations. The CPR and Great Northern were still slugging it out in Boundary County, but by 1919 the Phoenix mines were exhausted; the smelters were closed, and seemingly overnight the community became a ghost town. Finally, in 1912, cooler heads prevailed, and Great Northern and the CPR signed an agreement ending 30 years of hostilities between the two companies. Van Horne's vision for dominance in the Kootenays had prevailed, but he never lived to enjoy the day. James J. Hill passed away in 1916 and to the end never forgave Van Horne and the CPR for what he had considered "gross injustices," dating back to 1883.

In the 1920s, Great Northern announced an upgrade to the Nelson–Spokane passenger service, replacing the standard steam engine, mail car and coach configuration with a faster gasoline-electric rail car. The self-powered unit, affectionately called the "Galloping Goose," was most successful and well received, cutting the travel time to Spokane, as well as eliminating the cost of a complete train. But rail travel fell off sharply at the beginning of the Second World War, and in 1941, after 45 continuous years, the Spokane passenger train service ceased. But into the 1960s, the Great Northern system-wide timetable advertised a bus service with Greyhound from Nelson to Trail to Spokane, with connections to GN's main line trains.[52]

While GN's presence in the Kootenays diminished, Canadian Pacific prospered. Through the 1920s, the smelter in Trail was bursting at the seams. The steamboats could not keep up with the demand for ore from the Sullivan Mine in Kimberley, and a rail link from Kootenay Landing to Procter had to be secured. Tom Lymbery writes, "The deciding factor in closing the gap was the 1929 service disruption on the mainline when the Surprise Creek bridge collapsed in the Rogers Pass. One hundred percent of Canada's east-west traffic diverted to the southern mainline. All available tugs and sternwheelers were pressed into service around the clock to transfer passengers and express across the lake from Kootenay Landing to Procter. Rail cars shuttled on ferries and barges for the 30-mile stretch. The mainline was out of service for weeks, convincing the powers in the Montreal head office to complete the link. Contracts were let, and on January 31, 1931, CP completed the last link on the southern mainline."[53]

But for every action there is always an equal and opposite reaction. The rail link completed from Kootenay Landing to Procter, while in itself a significant achievement, began the slow decline of steamboat services on the lake. When the first train left Kootenay Landing for Procter, the Crow Boat and flagship of CP's fleet, the SS *Nasookin*, was out of a job. There was nowhere to reposition such a ship, with her elegant staterooms, fine dining and luxury parlours, plus the *Nasookin*'s size and

52   Schedule information courtesy Great Northern Railway Historical Society, Seattle Archives.
53   Lymbery, Tom's Gray Creek, Volume 1, 61.

capacity were excessive for the requirements of local runs. At the same time, all other CP lake boats were docked and placed out of service at Procter, except the SS *Moyie*, continuing to serve on the Kaslo and North Kootenay Lake run.

In the spring, the road from Creston to Gray Creek and Balfour to Nelson provided the CPR with the opportunity to initially lease and eventually sell the *Nasookin* to the provincial government for ferry service on the lake. Thus, in May of 1931, the *Nasookin* embarked on her second life as the Kootenay Lake ferry, three trips a day from Balfour to Gray Creek.

Looming on the horizon was another threat to the lake boats. The province was expanding the highway network into the interior. On July 28, 1926, the highway from Nelson to Kaslo officially opened with an Ainsworth ceremony. The head-line in the July 29, 1926, edition of the *Kootenaian* read: "His Honour, R. Randolph Bruce, Lieutenant Governor, Officially Opens Kaslo-Nelson Scenic Highway," with the sub-head-line, "Canada's Governor General Wires His Best Wishes For The Occasion."[54]

The article went on to describe the event:

> Kaslo citizens yesterday entertained one of the larg-est crowds in its history on the occasion of the official opening of the Kaslo–Nelson Scenic Highway...and Nelson and Trail citizens in particular, in addition to large numbers from intervening points turned out en masse, about three hundred and fifty coming up on the excursion boat from Nelson, Procter, Ainsworth and Riondel, in addition to about one hundred automobile

54   *Courtesy Kootenay Lake Historical Society, Kaslo,* BC.

loads from points far away as Quebec. Long before the scheduled hour of the official cutting of the barrier at Ainsworth, scores of cars were on hand at the old Ainsworth Camp. The crowd, augmented mainly by the arrival of the official party, included His Honour, R. Randolph Bruce and his niece, Miss Helen MacKenzie and Premier Oliver.

Promptly at 11 am, His Honour officially opened the road, Miss Helen MacKenzie untying the barrier, by that act intimating that highway communication was formally opened between Kaslo and Nelson and all parts of the continent. Premier John Oliver, who with Mrs. Oliver came for the opening of the road, replied, briefly, stating the great pleasure to be had in being present.

In an interview, Tom Lymbery said, "It was a rugged road, but by 1930 a small Nelson company called Canadian Greyhound Coaches, established in 1929 by George Fry and Speedy Olsen, began service to Kaslo, as well as Nelson to New Denver and eventually to Nakusp. The Nelson to Kaslo run was a challenge, especially in winter. However, in an emergency, the drivers had a key to a cabin at Coffee Creek, often the trouble spot, where the passengers and driver could wait out a storm or for help to arrive. With the commencement of the Kootenay Lake ferry service, Greyhound seized the opportunity to start a daily service from Nelson to Calgary and secured a Canada Post mail contract as well. This small company was the beginning of Greyhound Lines of Canada, and the Gray Creek Store became the East Shore agent."

Throughout the 1930s, Greyhound expanded its services in the Kootenays, Alberta and eventually to Vancouver, becoming a serious challenger to CP's regional transportation monopoly. In particular, Greyhound began to dominate the local market with frequent departures and professional service. For instance, the Nelson-Castlegar-Trail route was expanded to eight departures daily, making CP's once-daily service seem redundant.[55] In 1940 the little Nelson company that grew sold to Greyhound USA.

But CP in the Kootenays had an active operations centre in Nelson and was an agile company. Time and time again, local management proved its worth, reacting quickly to adverse situations and providing novel solutions to cut costs and services without violating its railway charters. For example, during the Depression, the economic activity in the Kootenays fell sharply as the prices of ore declined, closing many of the marginal mines, and exploration had come to a complete halt. With no work available, the population fell off. A great example of meeting the challenge was removing an entire train from the Lardeau to the Gerrard route, saving the expense of a whole crew without violating charter and provincial regulations. The solution? Replace the train with a motorized rail car that hauled a smattering of passengers and towed two freight wagons, thereby complying with service requirements.

However, Canadian Pacific had little or no competition on the long-haul passenger services. With the rail link from Kootenay Landing to Nelson operative, and ignoring the unfolding Depression, the Kootenay Express and the Kettle Valley Express began service on the southern main line. Canadian Pacific's transcontinental Train 1 provided the eastern Canada link, arriving in Medicine Hat at 4:45 pm, connecting to the Kootenay Express

55 Lymbery, Tom's Gray Creek, Volume 1.

for Nelson, Penticton and Vancouver at 5:15 pm. Similarly, the eastbound Kettle Valley Express arrived in Medicine Hat at 9:50 pm, linking to the eastbound Dominion to Winnipeg, Toronto and Montreal, departing at 10:40 pm. The Kootenay and Kettle Valley Express consisted of a first class coach, cafe parlour, first class sleeper and portions of the trip a dining car. A sleeper out of Calgary joined the train in Fort Macleod through to Nelson. At Yahk, BC, both trains connected with Spokane International's daily schedule to Bonners Ferry, Sandpoint and Spokane. By 1931, and the completion of the southern main line, Great Northern's presence in southern British Columbia had greatly diminished, leaving the CPR with little competition.

CP's Kootenay Lake service to Kaslo, Lardeau and Argenta, carrying cargo and passengers, continued to thrive. Highways and Greyhound had yet to appear at that end of the lake. The SS *Moyie* carried passengers and cargo; a small stable of tugs powered the rail barges. On Arrow Lakes, the West Robson to Arrowhead service initially had little disruption, and the route was served in summer by the SS *Bonnington* and the SS *Rossland*. But in the winter the SS *Minto* took over. The narrows between upper and lower Arrow Lakes were often ice-bound and the *Minto*, with her steel-reinforced hull and shallow draft, was better equipped for winter duty. But as the Great Depression deepened into the 1930s, Arrow Lakes passenger traffic suffered a sharp decline, and tourism numbers collapsed. The *Bonnington* was the pride of the fleet but was a massive boat with a large crew and expensive to power. So in 1931 CP withdrew her from service. From 1931 through 1954, the SS *Minto* and the screw tug *Columbia* maintained the Arrow Lakes schedules.

In addition to withdrawing the *Bonnington* from service, in 1932 the Robson to Arrowhead timetable was reduced to twice weekly sailings; northbound on Tuesdays and Fridays to Nakusp, southbound from Nakusp on Monday and Thursday. Nakusp to Arrowhead was a round trip sailing on Wednesdays and Saturdays. Connecting train service from Revelstoke to Arrowhead was similarly curtailed to twice weekly. Nakusp to Rosebery passenger service was a mixed train, twice weekly. The SS *Slocan* schedule from Rosebery to Slocan City, connecting to the mixed train to Nelson, was also chopped to twice-weekly sailings. On January 12, 1933, as reported in the *Kootenaian*, a massive slide resulted in the cancellation of train service between Kaslo and Sandon, causing CP to abandon the passenger schedule.[56] At a meeting on June 12, the Kaslo Board of Trade insisted that the CPR restore some service for the district. In response, a letter from Nelson Superintendent Manson intimated that it was not the intention of the company to run any regularly scheduled service on the railway that summer. Accordingly, the Kaslo to Sandon passenger service was abandoned.

The world descended into chaos on September 1, 1939, when the Second World War broke out. Canada was yanked out of the Depression as factories and industries changed direction to supply the war effort with the munitions and machinery required to fight Hitler's Germany. In 1941, after Japan's attack on Pearl Harbor, the war had become a global conflict. In the Kootenays, CP's smelter in Trail went into overdrive, increasing lead, zinc and silver production, and the freight traffic through the Kootenays soared with the increased production. Troop trains criss-crossed the country on both main lines as Canada responded to the call of war. But the war effort could not spare all Kootenay rail services. The predicted mining boom had

56   *Courtesy Kootenay Lake Archives, Kaslo, BC.*

never transpired around Trout Lake, and in 1942 CP abandoned the Kootenay & Arrowhead Railway from Lardeau to Gerrard. In April 1945, Germany surrendered, and in September the US Air Force dropped two atomic bombs on the Japanese cities of Hiroshima and Nagasaki, ending the war.

The Kootenays even played a role in the Manhattan Project, the massive effort to develop the A-bomb. This highly clandestine enterprise occurred in Trail, BC, led by Selwyn Blaylock, president of CP's Consolidated Mining & Smelting Company.

At the end of the war, Canada's economy began to falter as it geared down from wartime production and needed a boost to kick-start a peacetime economy. Over a million servicemen returned to civilian life, making jobs and housing top priorities. The Allies' Marshall Plan in Europe and the return to hostilities brought about by the Korean War provided short-term cures for exports. But massive federal and provincial government infrastructure projects created the real surge to full employment. Housing, highways and hydro became the mantra.

All was good news for the Canadian Pacific and the southern main line. The Trail smelter operated at capacity, feeding Canada's surging industrial landscape with metals required for the new peacetime economy. BC's timber industry ramped up to new levels, meeting the demands of a nationwide housing boom. In 1947 travellers and passenger revenues approached pre-Depression levels as tourism and business travel flourished. Once again, all was well in the Kootenays.

THE GOOD, THE BAD AND THE UGLY

While the '50s and '60s ushered in wealth and prosperity, storm clouds gathered in the Kootenays. The post-war era of unprecedented highway construction swept the nation in lockstep with the coming age of the automobile. Roads blanketed the province, and paved highways were slowly becoming the norm. The Trans-Canada Highway project began in the early 1950s, and trucking fleets expanded. By 1950 Greyhound had made significant inroads across southern British Columbia and Alberta.

Privately, CP was not always opposed to competition from Greyhound, often citing the increased competition as the rationale for abandoning passenger service on unproductive routes. The fact was Canada's railways were ditching unprofitable services all across the country. By 1950 CP had eliminated passenger trains on many branch lines connecting smaller communities, replacing them with bus connections, including Castlegar to Trail. But by 1952 frequent Greyhound schedules had begun to siphon off revenues from CP's passenger services through the Crowsnest Pass to Nelson. In a last valiant effort, Canadian Pacific struck back, announcing a new schedule for the Kettle Valley Express, as well as the introduction of a new overnight train.

Two simultaneous CPR press releases, dated April 18, 1952, announced,

> British Columbia's rugged, picturesque Coquihalla Pass on the Kettle Valley Line of the Canadian Pacific

Railway will be revealed to daylight rail travellers after April 27. According to an official announcement, the company will institute a new, improved schedule for the Kettle Valley Express, operating between Vancouver and Medicine Hat. A morning departure at 8:00 o'clock [*sic*] and a faster schedule will feature direct connections at Medicine Hat with the company's crack "Dominions," operating on main transcontinental routes to Toronto and Montreal. A "bonus" to travellers over the Kettle Valley–Crowsnest alternative route to the east will be the scenic 56-mile daylight run through the Coquihalla Pass and its series of spectacular views overlooking the Coquihalla River and the mountains through which the line operates. A new schedule for the route formerly travelled on overnight runs will feature through sleeping car service from Vancouver to Regina.[57]

The second CPR press release was dated the same day: "The Canadian Pacific has also announced that, commencing April 27, 1952, a new overnight train, to be referred to as 'No. 68,' will operate daily from Nelson through Lethbridge to Medicine Hat, with standard sleeper from Nelson to Calgary via Fort Macleod and will make connections at Medicine Hat with transcontinental train No. 2."

The announcement was well received and would be a boost for the local economy. As reported in the *Nelson Daily News*, on February 18, 1952, "New Canadian Railway schedules effective in Kootenay Division April 27 will see one train made up in Nelson. The new schedule under which two trains a day

57   *Courtesy Touchstones Museum of Art and History, Nelson, BC.*

will operate here was announced last week. Train No. 68 leaving at 5:00 pm daily, will originate at Nelson. It will arrive at Medicine Hat at 11:50 am the following day, and a split section will arrive at Calgary at 11:30 am. No. 67 arriving in Nelson at 11:45 am daily leaves Medicine Hat at 4:35 pm; the split section pulling out of Calgary at 7:40 pm."[58]

On April 29, the inaugural Train 67 brought a group of "Friendship Tourers" organized by the Lethbridge Chamber of Commerce. The same day *Nelson Daily News* reported, "A rollicking band of Southern Albertans stormed into town on No. 67's first run on Monday to receive an enthusiastic welcome and in turn give an uproarious demonstration of the widely known Alberta brand of goodwill. On a tour of the Kootenays, organized by Lethbridge Chamber of Commerce, a total of 105 men formed the group from the southern part of Alberta, who rode the first train to operate on the new Nelson–Medicine Hat CPR service."[59]

On December 18, 1952, Canadian Pacific announced, "73 New Diesels Ordered for Kootenay, Kettle Valley Runs." The report went on to specify, "More than a million and a half dollars has been earmarked by the Canadian Pacific Railway Company for the construction at Nelson, BC, of facilities for shopping and servicing diesel locomotives which will transform the company's service in southern British Columbia after delivery next year. The shop will be the second-largest of its kind in Canada. Made of steel and concrete with asbestos siding, it will be equipped with a 25-ton crane, plus all other facilities

58 *Courtesy Touchstones Museum of Art and History, Nelson, BC.*
59 *Courtesy Touchstones Museum of Art and History, Nelson, BC.*

necessary for the routine servicing of types of diesel locomotives."[60] Thus, 1952 continued to be a good year for enhancing Nelson's status as the primary divisional point.

"Nation's Most Modern Diesel Service Plant Opens in Nelson Today," the headline blared on January 29, 1954, in the *Nelson Daily News*: "Canadian Pacific Railway today will open its new diesel maintenance shop at Nelson. Mayor Joseph Kary will declare the facility officially open during public inspection of the new service plant this afternoon. The building is 305 feet long, covering two tracks, each accommodating a four-unit diesel locomotive. It also features two shorter tracks, a truck release track, administration offices, testing laboratory and workrooms."[61] Nelson had become a major CP maintenance centre in western Canada, second only to Ogden Shops in Calgary.

In April of 1955, Canadian Pacific launched the all new, streamlined, transcontinental "Canadian," designated trains 1 and 2. As a result, other services were renumbered, including the "stop everywhere" transcontinental Montreal to Vancouver service that had begun life as the Imperial Limited, then changed simply to trains 1 and 2 in the 1930s and now renumbered as trains 17 and 18. In addition, the Toronto sections of the Canadian trains 11 and 12 necessitated number reassignment to the Kootenay Express and the Kettle Valley Express to trains 67 and 68, commencing in the spring of 1955.

But hidden in the excitement of the Canadian announcement was some terrible news for Nelson. First, the hammer fell on the second Medicine Hat–Calgary–Nelson schedule.

60   *Nelson Daily News, December 19, 1952. Courtesy Touchstones Museum of Art and History, Nelson, BC.*
61   *Courtesy Touchstones Museum of Art and History, Nelson, BC.*

Having failed to increase ridership, it became a money-losing proposition. Moreover, as the train was based and marshalled in Nelson, it was the first noticeable hit to local railway jobs. Sadly, this action was a harbinger of things to come.

On October 27, 1957, Canadian Pacific made an even more devastating decision, cancelling the overnight sleeper service from Medicine Hat, Lethbridge and Nelson to Vancouver. This action ended the Kootenay Express and the Kettle Valley Express, which connected southern BC with Vancouver and eastern Canada through so many formative years. New highways, the increasing affordability of automobiles, the trucking industry and Greyhound had achieved what James J. Hill and the Great Northern Railway failed to do: they had the CPR on the run in the Kootenays.

CP continued limited passenger service with daylight operations between Medicine Hat and Vancouver. Budd Rail Diesel Cars required only two employees, replacing traditional full-set trains. Job losses were significant as full crews, including engineers, firemen, conductors, brakemen, car porters and dining car staff, were no longer required. Ticket offices were downsized or closed at many stations.

What is a Budd Rail Diesel Car?

The Budd Rail Diesel Car, RDC or Buddliner is a self-propelled diesel multiple unit (DMU) railcar. Between 1949 and 1962, 398 RDCs were built by the Budd Company of Philadelphia, Pennsylvania, United States. The cars were primarily adopted for passenger service in rural areas with low traffic density or short-haul commuter service and less expensive to operate in this context than a traditional diesel locomotive-drawn train with coaches. The cars could be used singly or coupled together in train sets and controlled from the cab of the leading RDC. Canadian Pacific purchased 53 cars. The first RDC arrived on November 9, 1954. CP used the RDCs, which it called Dayliners, throughout its system.[62]

The 1957 system-wide timetable introduced CP's Dayliner schedule.[63] Service was daily between Medicine Hat/Nelson and Penticton/Vancouver, but only twice weekly between Nelson and Penticton.

Daily, Medicine Hat–Nelson

LV: Medicine Hat, 9:10 am.
AR: Lethbridge, 11:20 am.
LV: Lethbridge, noon.
AR: Cranbrook, 4:15 pm.
LV: Cranbrook, 4:25 pm.
AR: Nelson, 8:55 pm.
LV: Nelson, 7:00 am.
AR: Cranbrook, 11:25 am.
LV: Cranbrook, 11:35 am.
AR: Lethbridge, 6:20 pm.
LV: Lethbridge, 6:30 pm.
AR: Medicine Hat, 8:30 pm.

62   "Budd Rail Diesel Car," Wikipedia, https://en.wikipedia.org/wiki/Budd_Rail_Diesel_Car.
63   Timetable courtesy Steve Boyko, www.traingeek.ca.

Mondays and Thursdays, Nelson–Penticton; Tuesdays and Fridays, Penticton–Nelson

LV: Nelson, 7:00 am.
AR: Penticton, 3:20 pm.
LV: Penticton, 8:00 am.
AR: Nelson, 4:15 pm.

Daily, Penticton–Vancouver

LV: Penticton, 3:30 pm.
AR: Vancouver, 10:40 pm.
LV: Vancouver, 8:00 am.
AR: Penticton, 3:05 pm.

CP's introduction of the Dayliners was a national strategy to dramatically cut costs on failing passenger services, many operating off the main line to less populated and rural destinations. By 1956 Canadian Pacific Airlines flew from Calgary to Cranbrook to Castlegar twice daily and expanded routes from Vancouver throughout the interior, including the Okanagan. However, CP had seen the future of travel in western Canada, and it didn't include passenger trains on the Crowsnest/Kettle Valley line.

The next blow to passenger service and the Kettle Valley Railway occurred on November 23, 1959: a massive mudslide washed out the line through Coquihalla Canyon. On November 28, CP announced the Coquihalla portion would remain closed until repairs were possible and all Kettle Valley Railway traffic would be rerouted through Merritt to the main line at Spences Bridge. For over a year, there were no updates or releases. Speculation was rife that the railway had had enough.

Then in January of 1961, confirming all fears, CP announced its intention not to re-open the line. On July 18, 1961, the government approved the request to abandon the line and remove the rails.[64] The railway through the Coquihalla was no more.

Canadian Pacific continued service from Penticton to Vancouver, rerouting the Dayliner north through Merritt to the main line at Spences Bridge, connecting to the Dominion to Vancouver. But it was a brutal schedule, departing Penticton at 8:00 pm, arriving in Vancouver at 7:45 am. The return was no better, departing Vancouver on the eastbound Dominion at 8:00 pm, connecting to the Dayliner at Spences Bridge in the middle of the night, arriving in Penticton at 8:20 am.[65]

Not only did the schedule add three hours to the trip but it was no longer a "same day" service. If the scheduling meant to chase passengers away, it worked brilliantly, as ridership tumbled, sometimes to single digits per trip. The writing was on the wall, and the CPR was determined to abandon the service.

With only twice-weekly Budd Rail Diesel Car service between Penticton and Nelson, ridership was always anemic but still showed a decline, from 11 in 1959 and ten in 1960, to seven in 1961 and just five in 1962. Between Nelson and Cranbrook, average ridership fell from 18 in 1959 and 14 in 1960 to 11 in 1961 and ten in 1962. Cranbrook to Lethbridge also saw a drop, from 19 in 1959 and 16 in 1960, to 14 in 1961 and 1962. These figures come from the Board of Transport Commissioners' report on CP's application in 1963 to discontinue trains 45–46 over the 761 miles between Lethbridge and Spences Bridge. CP cited

64   Sanford, *McCulloch's Wonder.*
65   *Schedule information from* CPR *Systemwide Timetable, 1960.*
Courtesy Steve Boyko, www.traingeek.ca.

a four-month survey of passenger traffic taken from January through April in 1962 and 1963, which showed that of the 125 stations along that route, fully 85 had seen no passengers boarding or alighting in those eight months. The railway stated that 1961 recorded gross revenue of $102,100 against gross expenses of $549,500, for a net deficit of $447,400. Revenue was almost entirely from passenger fares. Express and mail revenues were insignificant. In 1962 gross income had dropped to $86,100, while gross expenses rose to $596,100, for a net deficit of $510,000. In reviewing these figures, the Board of Transport Commissioners disallowed some expenses, reducing the total to $470,500, for a deficit of $385,000. Still, that was enough to sway the board to agree with CP's request, despite the hearings that brought out local politicians promoting daily service without the overnight stopovers. On October 23, 1963, the board ordered as follows: "The Canadian Pacific Railway Company, on or after the 16th day of January 1964, is authorized to discontinue the operation of trains 45 and 46 between Lethbridge, Alberta, and Spences Bridge, British Columbia, upon sixty days prior notice filed with the Board and posted in each railway station served by the said trains. The said notice shall also be published in one issue of a newspaper published or having general circulation in each of Fernie, Cranbrook, Creston, Nelson, Trail, Penticton, Princeton and Merritt."[66] All that remained was for the trains to make their final runs.

A series of articles in the *Nelson Daily News* in 1964 chronicled the demise of passenger service in the Kootenays. The January 15 edition highlighted a flashback to 1958. On February

66 *Canadian Railroad Historical Association,* "BC Budd," *Canadian Rail, March/April, 2009, 55–56.*

18, 1958, smiles were frequent on civic faces as the new Dayliner service of the CPR was inaugurated: "Trying out the reclining seats in the rail diesel car were Nelson Chamber of Commerce members and a company official....But, just a month short of its sixth birthday, the flower has faded from the bloom of the rail innovation. Today, January 15, marks the last Dayliner trip out of Nelson, ending more than half a century of railway passenger service."

The January 17 edition of the paper sported the headline: "Gary Higgs Last Off The Last Car From East." The article read, "Gary Higgs added a note to Nelson's history. The 20-year-old man from Nelson was the last person off the Dayliner from Lethbridge, which completed its last run to Nelson Thursday night, January 16, arriving right on schedule. Higgs was near the doorway when the other seven passengers began descending but patiently waited for the others to file by him and out into the crisp night air. Five minutes after depositing its passengers at the depot, the Dayliner was chugging towards the diesel shop; its job in the Kootenays finished."

The final article appeared on January 18 with the headline: "Caribou Pair Make Special Trip Here On Last Train." The article read, "Here she comes, a spectator yelled! And with three words, the last Dayliner arrived in Nelson via the Kettle Valley line from Penticton last night, marking the end of more than half a century of CPR passenger service in southeastern BC. The last train, which chugged into Nelson almost two hours late, left a happy impression on the memories of retired Cariboo ranchers, Mr. and Mrs. James Keefe of McLeese Lake. The only old-timers to ride the train from Spences Bridge to Nelson, the pair heartily agreed that this was the greatest little trip they had made in this country. In addition, W.A. Fetterley, President of the Nelson Museum Association, was the only Nelsonite to ride the train from Taghum to obtain the fifteen passengers' and crew's signatures so that the final ride would have some historical recognition in the Nelson Museum."[67]

On January 18, the three Dayliners operating the southern main line service were coupled together in Nelson and ran to Calgary on the regular Train 46 schedule, but no passengers were on board. Except for a few excursion trains over the years, these were the last passenger trains through the Nelson station.

The unthinkable had happened. Passenger service on the southern main line was gone forever, and the glory of the once famous and contentious route was being hacked up and dissected like a grisly post-mortem. The Kettle Valley Railway continued to shrink, and small trackside communities fell by the wayside as the new economy made the southern main line redundant.

The termination of passenger service to Nelson marked the beginning of the end for the classic railway town of the interior. In the early 1960s, few would have predicted that Nelson's divisional point and diesel repair shop would ever close. Or that the Nelson train station, the hub of the community for over 70 years, would fall into disuse and slowly rot away. But happen it did, as the startling changes in the 1970s and '80s ended divisional status and devastated Nelson's economy. The trains of the Kootenays ruled no more.

67 All Nelson Daily News articles courtesy Touchstones Museum of Art and History, Nelson, BC.

EPILOGUE

THE END OF A DREAM

Against James J. Hill's wishes, the signing of the Coquihalla Agreement in 1912 ended the Great Northern's forays into Canada. The Great Depression of the 1930s saw the removal of most tracks. However, Great Northern continued to pay its trackage rights and maintenance fees through the Coquihalla until the 1930s. It finally negotiated an exit agreement with the CPR, abandoning all rights and claims to the line. Canadian Pacific had finally achieved its mission: to dominate the transportation landscape in the Kootenays and southern British Columbia.

The completion of the Kettle Valley Railway through the Coquihalla had brought joy to both politicians and citizens alike. But for Canadian Pacific it may have been a pyrrhic victory; the cost to maintain the Coquihalla line was so expensive it was tantamount to defeat. For 45 years, upkeep proved to be a financial sinkhole. As much as 50 to 60 feet annually, heavy snowfall resulted in massive avalanches and washouts, often closing the line for months at a time. During many years of operation, the CPR abandoned the line in the winter months to face costly repair bills in the spring. On top of the maintenance expenses, the Coquihalla route was the most expensive rail line ever constructed in North America. It is doubtful the CPR even came close to amortization.

But the last "spike" in the Kettle Valley coffin was the changing economic landscape in the transportation business.

Competitive railways mustered longer trains, led by more powerful diesel locomotives. Longer trains also meant operating fewer schedules, saving on crew labour, fuel and locomotives. With new technology, freight trains on the main line had become 100-plus cars long, but trains of that length were not possible on the southern route. From Castlegar through to Hope, many grades were well over the accepted railway maximum of 2.2 per cent. The required pusher locomotives meant extra crews and more fuel consumption.

Additionally, the snaking of the line through river canyons and over high mountain passes created tight curves, far too tight for longer trains to navigate. Thus, the Kettle Valley Railway evolved from a patriotic dream to a bean counter's nightmare. As the Canadian Pacific Railway began the transition away from "Canada's Company" to corporate North America, the romance of the rails was fast disappearing into CP's history.

In 1968, as part of a corporate reorganization, each of CP's primary operations was organized as a separate subsidiary, including its rail operations.[68] The name of the railway was changed to CP Rail, and the parent company changed its name to Canadian Pacific Limited in 1971. The air, express, telecommunications, hotel and real estate holdings were spun off, and all companies transferred to Canadian Pacific Investments.

The dominos began falling. The following summarizes the demise of the Kootenay railways:

68   "Canadian Pacific Railway," Wikipedia, https://en.wikipedia.org/ wiki/Canadian_Pacific_Railway#:~:text=Donald%20Smith%2C%20 later%20known%20as,of%20BC's%20entry%20into%20Confederation.

- On November 23, 1959, a massive mudslide washed out the line through Coquihalla Canyon. After five days of mixed messages, a November 28 statement from CP announced the Coquihalla portion would remain closed until repairs were possible. All Kettle Valley Railway traffic would be rerouted through Merritt to the main line at Spences Bridge.

- In January of 1961, confirming all fears, CP announced its intention not to re-open the Coquihalla line.

- On July 18, 1961, the government approved the request to abandon the line and remove the rails, eliminating the subdivision.

- In 1964 passenger service was abandoned.

- In May of 1973, the rail line closed between Penticton and Beaverdell.

- In 1973 the Canadian Locomotive Company–built Fairbanks Morse locomotives were retired, and the Nelson diesel shop closed in 1974.

- In 1978 CP received permission to abandon the entire section of track between Penticton and Midway, marking the beginning of the onslaught of abandonment in the Kootenays.

- On December 20, 1988, the rail car ferry on Slocan Lake to Rosebery and the train to Nakusp made their last runs.

- In 1988 BNSF abandoned the Nelson & Fort Sheppard rail line from Nelson through Salmo to Fruitvale. All that remains is the ATCO Wood Products short line from Fruitvale to the Columbia Gardens Interchange, about ten kilometres long, named the Nelson & Fort Sheppard Railway Corporation.

- The final indignity was the abandonment of the rail line between Midway and Castlegar in 1990. Except for the line from Castlegar to the Cominco smelter in Trail, the Columbia & Western Railway was gone.

The Kootenay railways quietly disappeared into the dustbin of history. Was the expenditure of millions of dollars in the race to the coast all for naught? Apparently not for the Province of British Columbia, for the following reasons:

- The fierce competition accelerated the construction of railways in the Kootenays (and all across southern BC) between 1891 and 1912, providing the mines and forest industry of the southern interior access to hungry manufacturers in Canada and the United States.

- The railways established fledging communities and industries that grew into tax-paying cash machines for the government.

- For over 50 years, the railway networks provided the umbilical cord connecting the interior communities with Vancouver and Spokane.

- The duplication of railways to towns and mines led to fiercely competitive rates, benefitting the shippers and the travelling public.

- Canadian raw materials could be shipped across Canada and throughout British Columbia, halting much of the flow of goods and capital south to the United States.

Both railways are now far beyond the Battle of the Kootenays. Great Northern, now BNSF, has become the largest railway in North America, and the Canadian Pacific the most successful railway in Canada. While both railways maintain trackage in Canada and the United States, they are friendly competitors, with many interline exchanges. A small part of the southern main line continues to exist, thriving on freight traffic. CP's Crowsnest line still hauls millions of tons of coal annually to this day. The Kootenay branch line transports thousands of tons of silver, lead, zinc and fertilizer from the Teck smelter (formerly CP's Consolidated Mining & Smelting Company) in Trail, BC.

For over 30 years, the railway communities of British Columbia's Kootenays witnessed one of the greatest battles for supremacy ever seen on the continent. It was an exciting, turbulent chapter in the building of the province. It is a saga for the nation's bookshelves.

SELECTED SOURCES

Burrows, Roger G. *Railway Mileposts: British Columbia, Volume II: The Southern Route from the Crowsnest to the Coquihalla.* West Vancouver: Gordon Soules Book Publishers Ltd., 1981.

"Canadian Pacific Railway, 1881–1975." *Timetable World.* https://timetableworld.com/ttw-viewer?token=e25f-29cd-61ce-47a4-b8c8-ae5eaae2ed6f.

Canadian Railroad Historical Association. "BC Budd." *Canadian Rail*, March/April, 2009.

———. "The Crowsnest Pass." *Canadian Rail*, Issue 453, July–August 1996.

"The Crowsnest Line." *Atlas of Alberta Railways.* https://railways.library.ualberta.ca/Chapters-7-4/.

den Otter, A.A. *Bondage of Steam: The CPR and Western Canadian Coal.* Vancouver: Douglas & McIntyre, 1984.

Doyle, Ted. "1905 Oriental Limited." *Ted's Great Northern Homepage.* https://www.gnflyer.com/1905OL.html.

Fahey, John. *Inland Empire: D.C. Corbin and Spokane.* Seattle: University of Washington Press, 1965.

Garden, J.F. *Nicholas Morant's Canadian Pacific.* Revelstoke, BC: Footprint Publishing, 1999.

Halbrook, Stewart. *James J. Hill: A Great Life in Brief*. Kenmore, WA: Epicenter Press, 2018.

Harris, Cole. "Moving amid the Mountains, 1870–1930." *BC Studies*, no. 58 (Summer 1983).

Harvey, R.G. *Carving the Western Path*. Victoria: Heritage House Books, 1998.

Hungry Wolf, Adolf. *Rails in the Canadian Rockies*. Skookumchuck, BC: Canadian Caboose Press, 1993.

Luebke, Emory. "Soo Line Schedules, Soo-Pacific, 1902, Soo-Spokane-Portland Train Deluxe, 1908." *Soo Line Historical and Technical Society*. www.sooline.org.

Lymbery, Tom. *Tom's Gray Creek, Volume 1*. Gray Creek, BC: Gray Creek Publishing, 2013.

———. *Tom's Gray Creek, Volume 2*. Gray Creek, BC: Gray Creek Publishing, 2016.

McDonald, J.D. *The Railways of Rossland British Columbia*. Trail, BC: Hall Printing, 1991.

"Montana Lines." *GNRHS & NPRHA Archives*. www.gn-np-jointarchive.org.

Norris, John. *Historic Nelson: The Early Years*. Lantzville, BC: Oolichan Books, 1995.

"Railway Wars in the Kootenays." *The Creston Museum*. https://crestonmuseum.ca/railway-wars-in-the-Kootenays/.

Ramsey, Bruce. *Ghost Towns of British Columbia*. Vancouver: Mitchell Press, 1963.

Riegger, Hal. *The Kettle Valley and Its Railways*. Vancouver: Evergreen Press, 1993.

Sanford, Barrie. *McCulloch's Wonder: The Story of the Kettle Valley Railway*. Vancouver: Whitecap Books, 1988.

Taylor, Bill, and Jan Taylor. *Rails to Gold and Silver*. Missoula, MT: Pictorial Histories Publishing Company, Inc., 1999.

Turner, Robert D. *The S.S. Moyie: Memories of the Oldest Sternwheeler*. Victoria: Sono Nis Press, 1991.

Turner, Robert D., and Davis S. Wilkie. *The Skyline Limited*. Victoria: Sono Nis Press, 1994.

ABOUT THE AUTHOR

In 1948 Terry's father, Frank Gainer, was transferred to Banff as the station agent. Part of the employment package was the agent's residence on top of the station where the family lived until 1955, when Mr. Gainer retired. Beginning in 1957, Terry worked seven summers at the station, initially as a porter in the baggage room and then as a redcap through the summer of 1962, the year of the Seattle World's Fair. Life at the Banff train station nurtured a lifelong passion for trains and railways.

Largely influenced by his upbringing, Terry has enjoyed a career that has been an amazing 50-year adventure in tourism. Terry officially retired in 2005 but has stayed involved in the industry as a planning and marketing consultant. In 2017 Terry began work on his first book, *When Trains Ruled the Rockies*, published in 2019. The first edition sold out in 2021 and the second edition will be released in May of 2022. But he still wasn't done with trains. In early 2021, Terry began work on this, his second book, *When Trains Ruled the Kootenays*. Terry resides in Kaslo, BC.